The Reluctant Country Boy

Vol. One

The following is a series of 'scream of consciousness' social media posts which I wrote somewhere between January 2021 and March 2022. This is a random time line because I'm not exactly sure, but it's there or thereabouts.

People seemed to like them and I have a bit of a following here and there but because I kind of prised my way in to various little groups where I didn't really belong I'm yet to find my true audience and that's why I've complied this little collection. Plus it's all original and as much as I don't mind folks sharing my stuff, the least they can do is reference me. If you ever see an old man walking down the street, arm in arm with a beautiful woman, rest assured it was almost certainly my words that made this happen. The cheeky bastards. One can't blame the fuckers though and if I wasn't me I'd be doing the same.

I have largely left the content as they first appeared but not in the same sequential order just to make the whole thing more anarchic. I love a bit of anarchy, especially from the comfort of my home. My advice would be to pick a page at random and then read for a bit then go and do something else. You can read it all in one go through if you want. You choose. It's not like an album or a Hollywood film, where there's a beginning and a middle and an end, so don't get all lineal about it and start trying to bite your own ears off.

It would have been easy for me to have edited them all in order to sex them up a bit more but I wanted to leave them as they were because at the time my rule was to start a sentence with a memory or idea and then just bash away for ten minutes and then press send.

One day I plan to write them into one long, beautifully grafted story but right now I just want to document them. Punctuation and grammar exist here and there but it wasn't my top priority because I wanted to write them like I was telling them to someone face to face. In my experience in real life we aren't all so coherent and eloquent as authors would have us believe and most conversations I have with people seem to go off on many different tangents and sometimes have no punch line at all and just get left hanging; sometimes forever.

All the stories are true but I have changed some names here and there to protect some people's identity as I wouldn't like to embarrass anyone; especially Steve who can be a right handful if provoked. I hope you find a few laughs here and there.

Enjoy.

Kind regards, Best wishes,

And thanks in advance, Sorry for your loss.

Dom xxx

Back in the eighties I had a mate who could never get laid. This was great and took the pressure off the rest of us. Anyway we were all village kids and this friend of mine- who shall remain nameless to protect his identity; oh go on then his name was Steve. Steve was an only child and unlike the rest of us had everything his heart desired; including one of those cool chopper bikes with the long handle bars and gears, the full cricket gear including stumps, pads and gloves and new clothes and shoes and football boots and also parents who were still together. He was a spoilt little bastard but I always liked him because he made me laugh and he was clearly a bit mental.

These days he'd have been looked at by a head doctor and been classified as being on the spectrum but back then he was just known to be a bit of a header.

I've seen him smash cricket bats around the heads of anyone who had the brass neck to bowel him out during a match and then tearfully take all his gear home with him in a right fucking tantrum; and as for some reason he never vented his frustrations out on me I always found this to be hilarious. The best thing about Steve was that he never gave one flying fuck about consequences and authority. One time while lining up for a class the head master walked by and as we were all being loud and unruly he stopped and attempted to bollock us. Unfortunately for him he picked on Steve who promptly told him to go and fuck himself. This defiant act resulted in gasps of astonishment all round. Inexplicably our head just stared at him for a moment in disbelief and then walked on. If I, or anybody else, had said this I know for a fact that we'd have got a detention and a

4

suspension and also a clip round the ear or the cane. Corporal punishment was still a thing back then and any misdemeanour was gleefully punished physically. Nobody had to sit on the stairs and think about what they'd done at my school no sir, they'd usually get a passing blow to the head or a dead arm. Job done.

Our metal teacher used to throw my mate about by his hair until one day he came in with a crew cut and as he could no longer get a good purchase instead he banged my mate's head repeatedly down onto a metal block. We didn't even question this behaviour at the time although later I must admit to my shame that via friends reunited I once offered out my old music teacher in the bit that said 'memories of your teachers' where I retold the time he pulled my ear so hard I heard it crack and if I ever ran in to him he'd be getting the same treatment.

One doesn't forget these things and often when I hear about some retired teacher being found bludgeoned in his kitchen I just assume it's a revenge attack. Our other metal work teacher got done for spying on kids going to the toilet in our local Keymarket's public toilet. This was a shame because I always got on with him and he had kids that went to the same school.

Anyway back to Steve. I don't want to draw this out because one thing that irks me more than most is when one of you take the time to write, 'too long to read' or 'that's five minutes I'll never get back' or some other witty bollocks that you think is the first time I've ever seen that. So I'll press on. Where was I? Oh yeah Steve's lack of getting any attention from what we used to simply call back in the day, girls. Let's jump to the time when he was 18 and the rest of us used to go drinking and clubbing. Steve was a keen skittle and darts player and was even in various pub teams but unfortunately for Steve these weren't your typical places to meet any single females under about fifty. He was an old soul and he didn't like dancing or fashion or the latest music so he was pretty much fucked. I can picture him now shuffling his feet self-consciously from side to side to the sounds of Wham and Duran- Duran pissed up but not enough to have a go at the time warp. I'm really aware of how long this is now so what I'm going to do is stop and maybe do a part two later. I can't really do one of those, feel good 'it's been two days since I've quit heroin' posts or my cat just climbed in the fridge ones, mine are all past memories of loons I used to know. If anyone cares remind me but for now I'm off because I don't want to upset the guy who after telling me that he hadn't learnt anything from one of my last long posts for some reason then called me a 'kiddy fiddle' which didn't really make a lot of sense but I could tell it wasn't a compliment. Fuck me is that the time?

Come on then let's put this Steve not getting laid saga to bed now shall we? That's a rhetorical question by the way. Honestly some folks after they've had a few drinks. I'm not in competition with anyone in here and I write these just for fun and for my own, and hopefully, your, entertainment.

The thing I don't want is for anyone to think that I'm stringing this out just for fun and to be known as some kind of textual prick teaser so I don't want this particular one to be just a filler. I remember buying queen's, hit single, I want to break free, back in the day and the B-side was an instrumental of the same song which I thought was a cheap shot and since that day I promised myself never to do the same thing to anyone else because I didn't want anyone to feel how let down I felt on that day.

Right then. Down to business. I most point out that I bought that little 45 rpm record before knowing that Queen played sun city in South Africa during apartheid and if I had there would be no way I would have done that. To this day I feel extremely guilty when I buy my mum Cliff Richard's latest calendar or book or CD because although he is a national treasure and was very handsome back in the day that little rascal along with Rod Stewart did the same thing. But let's move on. One thing I admired about Steve was that he never tried to make his life sound better than it was. While the rest of us were lying about how young we were when we lost our virginity (I was ten but I was a catholic choir boy so I was regarded in the trade as a late starter) I don't think it even occurred to Steve to embellish his love life and this was rather endearing even when he got into his

7

twenties. He did love a wank though and most Friday nights down the pub he'd regale me with all the previous ones he'd had since we'd last met and who were the lucky protagonists of said wanks.

Steve was a nut case but he always had enough respect for me never to mention my two sisters though and I was grateful for that because my sisters were regarded by many a lad as hot as fuck back then. He didn't have any siblings but if he did I like to think that if he had a sister and she was absolutely gorgeous of course I'd bash one out while thinking about giving her one but I would never have told him. A gentleman's agreement if you will.

His mum was a bit dumpy for my tastes and I'm ashamed to say never entered into any of my teenage MILF fantasies. They weren't called MILFS or cougars back then they were just called Randy old women who looked like they were up for it. Don't forget double standards weren't invented until at least the nineties. One of my favourite stories he told me was the one where he was lying on his bed and having a quick one off the wrist while watching his neighbour sun bathing in her garden. A classic, but the twist was that he was using his open window as a kind of transparent mirror so he didn't even need to hide behind the curtains he could just lay on his bed and pull his little pudding to his heart's content and his bollocks were empty. It was apparently a perfect angle and out of all of this sordid yet admittedly titillating tale (his neighbour was a lesbian which was very unusual at the time because lesbianism didn't really hit the west county with any real force until June 89 when CND came to town) the only thing that occurred to him afterwards that

8

might be fucked up about the whole scenario was that he couldn't work out if as he could see her could she see him and was she getting off on watching him wanking off while watching her? I've thought about this a great deal over the years and as I'm no good at that sort of thing, angles and mirrors and what have you I still don't have a fucking clue. I'm fairly certain that rather than finding the whole thing sexy if she'd caught him my gut instinct tells me she would have cut off his fucking nuts. Oh dear me once again we didn't get there did we? That's another rhetorical question. The trouble with writing these things straight off the cuff is that I never know where they're going until they've got there. I can only apologise once more and I can tell you that the next one will tie up all the loose ends and answer all your questions. Unless I get distracted obviously. I'm off.

Right then it's snowing here and I've got nothing better to do so put another log on the fire and a shawl on your legs and let's finally put you all out of your misery regarding my old mate Steve. But before I do I want to talk about drug use in the 80s when you live in the sticks. There was fuck all drugs to be had. There was alcohol and fags obviously copious amounts of these two but if you fancied experimenting with weed then you were pretty much fucked.

Once my balls had dropped and my dick got bigger I found living in a village stifling to say the least and dreamed of one day leaving never to return but until that time came I had to just grin and bear it. I lived in London with my mum and dad and sisters until they split up and then I was fostered for a bit then eventually, thank fuck, I was given to my Nan and that's where I stayed until she died. I was about 18 or 19 and the pain of her dying is with me to this day and just as raw and it's taken me up until very recently to get over her loss which sounds pathetic but there you go. I loved her with a fucking fury because she had saved me from my shitty childhood and she gave me stability. That pain was so awful I decided that I didn't have the strength to love anybody like that ever again so all the relationships I had were fleeting and superficial. Even the long ones I kept something back just in case it all went tits up which it invariably did and when I broke up with a girl or she broke up with me I was always happy that it had come to an end because it all seemed like a right royal pain in the arse most of the time. I only liked the initial hook up when everyone is on their best behaviour plus I didn't want to get a girl pregnant and then have to marry her and be trapped in village forever. That's how I saw it anyway.

When you live in a village you go out with girls more because they were local than because you were desperately in love with them and the numbers were limited. If you pulled a girl from a club or pub in town you couldn't just swap numbers like now and we didn't even have a home phone so you'd just have to hope she was in the same place at the same time the next week or whenever you could arrange to go back so luck always played a part. Steve on the other hand was still desperate to find a girlfriend but not enough to change his routine so in many ways he was his own worst enemy. He was happy to have a few pints on a Friday and Saturday night in one of our locals but because his cows needed milking early in the morning he couldn't stay out all night and get proper fucked up like the rest of us. I remember loads of occasions when I was convinced that I was going to die because I was so drunk and the hangovers were shocking. Oh yeah drugs I think the majority of lads I used to hang around with thought that drugs were evil and that if you had one toke on a spliff the next thing you'd know was that you were sucking off tramps to pay for your heroin habit but not me I knew that if I could get hold of any I'd fucking love them and I was right.

I did an apprenticeship as a painter and decorator and this brought a thicko like me into collage. Happy days. This was the first time that I could choose my friends rather than be friends with someone just because we were the same age and came from the same village or went to school with each other. Here you could have a good conversation about music with likeminded people and they could also turn you on to new bands and the place was full of girls.

 Steve never went to collage so he was once again fucked. Or not fucked to be more accurate. I hate bad puns but I'll swallow that one for the sake of continuity. So yeah even though most of the proper students looked down on us manual workers there was still ample opportunities for a cheeky little bastard like me to enjoy himself and access to girls and drugs became a bit easier. I say drugs we only ever smoked black Lebanese or red Lebanese hashish and it always tasted of petrol to me. I remember being given some off this kid and taking it home and rolling a joint and then sitting on a wall for about three hours thinking that it hadn't worked.

I'm not the best person to put anyone off taking drugs because in the main I've always had a great time. The first time I took magic mushrooms I truly believe I became enlightened and that experience changed me forever. I remember laying on my bed laughing my head off and knowing the answer to the universe and God and everything I even thought about writing it down but because it was so obvious I didn't bother. I woke up the next day and had forgotten it which still irks me. Top tip don't look into mirrors on shrooms. This is a big no no. I did and the devil himself stared right back at me but luckily for me my brain went, fuck off devil you're just a hallucination, and fuck off he did the malevolent looking mother fucker. I think that trip made me a better person because my lasting feeling was that as everything was connected then if I hurt someone or something I'd be hurting myself on some level so I've always tried to be nice unless someone is a real cock end then that goes out of the window but that's very rare.

We'd all heard about E of course but we were miles from that kind of life that came a few years later for me but one thing I knew was that I had to get the fuck out of dodge and as soon as my Nan died that's what I did. Steve stayed though because lots of people love the village life. When your Mum lives up the road and your sister and brother live down the road and your aunty lives over there and your cousins are over there it's nice but I found it claustrophobic and suffocating.

I packed a rucksack and fucked off abroad and was gone for three years and when I popped back for a catch-up I swear to you now that my mates were telling me stories that I already knew; that's how dull it was. I did meet up with Steve for a drink though and he told me that he'd also been abroad on holiday and he'd met someone while he was away ... I don't have a log burning stove but if I did I'd throw another one on and continue this story but I don't so I'm not going to right now but I think we've made a bit of progress. Shame really because the next bit is the best bit…

Kids are cruel. That's a fact. They haven't yet been socialised and bent into the shape of whichever society they were born in. Why are there so many child soldiers fighting wars? I think it's because they're more easily persuaded to do mad things like put their life at risk for a cause that most experienced folks would be saying, nah you're alright I'll just stay here and you fight your own wars, see ya later. You don't get many old suicide bombers unless they've been forced under gun point or had their family held hostage because the older one gets the more one thinks, nah fuck that I'm staying in tonight. Well because Steve had all the gear and the doting parents of an only child he clearly never felt the need to fit in or be socialised and made up his own rules.

 A kid does something wrong and gets told off and then typically they get punished so they understand the consequences of their actions which is fair enough. But if a kid never gets punished they don't have any boundaries and if there's no boundaries if you're an observer and they're not your kid then this can be loads of fun to watch. I was fascinated by Steve because my Nan brought me up and she was very strict and there was fucking loads and loads of rules so to see Steve doing whatever he liked all of the time was sexy as fuck. Don't get me wrong I didn't want to be him because he clearly had a good couple of screws loose and a shit hair cut but I've always been attracted to eccentrics and for some reason they always seem to find me and want to sit next to me and start being odd as fuck. I think it's because so called normal people have never interested me at all and they kind of scare me. Sometimes I'll be on a bus or a train and overhear a conversation that's so dull and full of platitudes that I think that they're being ironic. Good Morning. Good Morning. Nice day today. Yes. Did you sleep well? Not too bad did you sleep well? Did you see Ant and Dec last night? No I don't like them. Sorry guys but I couldn't help but overhear your conversation and I think it's better for all concerned if I shoot you both in the head just in case you're thinking of having kids. I know it's only politeness and once they get home they're probably going to be sticking stuff up their arseholes while wearing double denim and listening to Hitler speeches but I'm a dreamer and I want everyone to be more nutty when they're out and about like our Steven.

Years ago when I lived in London Town I was doing a degree in Barking east London but lived in Harrow on the hill which was west London (I really lived in Northolt but that sounded shit to tell people so I always said Harrow on the Hill) it was only a five minute walk up to their posh boys school though and being a massive leftie at the time I used to walk into Harrow via the route where I had to pass it just because I wanted to harass the little bastards. This was unintentional at first but when I realised that because they were all wearing little straw hats and blazers and had wanky little names, for some reason it was me that had to step into the road when they went from one part of their school to another - I never did formulate the collective noun for a gang of little Tory boys- I just called them that still oh so powerful c word. I can see them now striding down the road in their little huddles all pleased with themselves and full of fucking optimism. Don't get me wrong these twats were also products of their society and I didn't blame them individually for being so obnoxious but I did delight in holding my ground on the pavement as they assumed because I wasn't one of them that I'd naturally bow deeply in servitude as I stepped into the road to let them pass. Not me no sir I was a chest puffed out head high get the fuck out of my way red wedge chip on his shoulder socialist mother fucker taking up the whole space. I was like a communist Moses parting the waves to let my people through to the Promised Land which was in my case was the record shop on the top of that hill. Move aside you chinless wonders I'm off my nut on cheap speed and I need to buy some Neil young before I crash. The owner of that record shop was terrified of me and rightly so.

Oh yeah so because I had a two hour tube ride from west London to east London I had many an adventure with my fellow commuters. I was coming back one night and heard a commotion in the next carriage due to some drunken fucker. The next thing I know this young guy comes into my carriage which was empty apart from me. He sits opposite me and starts banging on about how this guy was drunk and frightening everyone and I'm just nodding and being polite than he says that he's a homosexual from Afghanistan and they aren't too keen on homosexuality in Afghanistan so he had to move here and I said yes that was for the best because although the UK wasn't by any means perfect we, as a nation, were more embracive than a lot of others. This was in the nineties and before everyone started hating each other. Well this guy then asked if I had a problem with gay people and of course I said yes and kicked his fucking head in. I didn't really I said of course not because I'm not a fucking wanker then he asked if he could sit next to me and I said he was fine where he was and then he asked me if I wanted a blow job and to be honest I did think about that because a blow job is a blow job but he had a beard and stank of body odour so I thanked him because I was genuinely flattered but declined his generous offer. I also thought about the cameras on the train and didn't want to be part of the tube drivers Christmas compilation tape in case I ever got famous even though the last thing I ever wanted to be was famous. Uh oh spaghetti oh I've only gone and went off on another mad tangent laugh out loud. Never mind I'm now writing for all those folks that need a distraction from their everyday existence and enjoy these little asides. I'm more than happy to put up with the too long to readers and the zzzz brigade and the 'I gave up after the first sentence' (this is why my sentences are so long to give myself a fighting chance with the hecklers

So Steve wasn't having much luck with the girls and as we got older he was having the same amount of luck with the ladies but the lad pressed on. Steve was a milker and I don't mean that he would lactate on hearing a crying baby no Steve's job was to put clusters on the udders of cows and their juice would come out of their massive nipples and get sucked up into pipes and then other stuff would happen until a tanker came to get it.

I never really cared or understood what the process was. I was a country boy but farming never interested me. Sometimes me and a few other kids would help out in the summer loading bales of hay onto the back of trailers in the searing heat and we'd swig warm and weak orange squash and my hands would get blistered and my Irish skin would turn pink. Sun cream wasn't invented back then and we just burned and then peeled and then burned again and calamine lotion was soothing for the first second it was dabbed on but then would dry out and make everything much worse. Steven fucking loved it though and I think that's why he had such a cavalier attitude to school and giving a fuck because his destiny was already mapped out.

He was the teenage boy driving a tractor along the motor way doing ten miles an hour and holding up all the holiday makers heading to Devon and Cornwall and he wasn't the kind of lad to pull over into a lay-by and let you pass. He was laughing his fucking head off. Sometimes he'd indicate left or right for a bit just to give the tourists behind him false hope then continue on straight indefinitely. I loved this about him. Even today if I see a tractor two miles ahead of me followed by ten million irate cars I always smile because I know that when I eventually get past the wanker there will be a grinning teenager driving it hopefully topless showing a perfect v shaped back with bulging arms and a six pack ... the sweat dripping off his torso and gleaming in the sunshine, wearing nothing but tight shorts and muddy Wellington boots ... where was I? Oh yeah As I said Farming wasn't for me and I think this was because my mum used to date one of the farmer's son's back in the day until he got another girl pregnant and had to marry her. They always kept in touch though and part of me always suspected that I was more than likely this fucker's kid too which made everything very awkward but this isn't about me it's about Steve and his quest to lose his virginity. I don't want to string this story out and waste everyone's precious time so I'm going to get straight to it. Steven didn't have a clue how to pull a girl none of us did really it wasn't like today when you could just google it and watch a YouTube video of some trendy dickhead telling you all about how easy it is to get laid if you just follow his tips and subscribe to his very sinister channel, it was trial and error. Steve used to hang out with his dad a lot and was happier in the company of adults such as his darts and skittle team even though they'd obviously rip the piss out of him for not having a girlfriend. It was never assumed that he must be gay which was unusual because that seemed to be the biggest insult that you could throw around back then. I never understood that though because if anything it was a compliment. The gay people I knew back then which was absolutely no one except this one boy in my year who seemed to me to be cool as fuck and was always surrounded by girls. We were in the changing room once and two boys in my year started to give him shit for having an earring and being camp and he lost it and bitch slapped the shit out of both of them and that's true and the look on their faces was priceless.

I was always glad that I wasn't an arsehole like those two pricks. I've never felt it to be any of my business who anyone else fancied or didn't fancy. I don't know if it's because I was brought up by my Nan and my mum and my sisters and I didn't have a bigoted dad around indoctrinating me with mad macho shit but for whatever reason other people's sexuality was none of my concern. I was unknowingly pretty camp myself to be honest. Still am given half a chance, or even a quarter of a chance but this isn't about me this is about Steve. I will quickly mention Steve's dad though because to me he was a legend. Back in the day our local had a skittle ally around the back and this was also used as a function room where we'd all have our 18th birthday discos (not me though I was too shy and didn't think anyone would come)and that sort of thing and it also had a piano in it and after playing skittles on a Friday I'd they were home Steve's dad would be pissed as a fart and start playing it and everyone else would singalong and to me this was the highlight of the night even if I'd fingered someone earlier. You don't get pianos in pubs so much these days and for me that's a shame because I love a drunken singsong.

... So we left Steve at the club unsuccessfully getting laid. The great thing about Steve, apart from his aversion to authority, was his honesty. Well this was a good thing unless you were on the receiving end of it of course. Steven could look into your soul and pull out all your insecurities and then parade them up and down the street while you crumbled inside. You had to have a quick wit and a thick skin if you ever felt like taking the piss out of him because he could destroy you. Our French teacher was called miss Higgins and we all liked her because she was pretty and nice and didn't hit us and all we had to do was copy what she wrote on the board into our French books because our class was deemed thick as shit and that's all we were capable of. This was a fair assessment to be honest. Sometimes she'd say a phrase and then point at one of us and then we'd repeat it and she'd say, 'excellent' in French which meant excellent and we'd be all pleased with ourselves and she would beam at us and sometimes her nipples would get hard under her blouse. My seat was centre stage right at the front and most of my time was spent thinking about her and the fitter of the two female PE teachers at it- sexism and objectifying women hadn't yet been invented so I didn't even think twice about it- or sometimes we'd ask for a pencil or a ruler in French which was the more advanced stuff. Even though somebody would ask for a ruler every single lesson we would all laugh are heads off because we thought that 'regle' meant period as in menstruation. The girls would blush and the boys would snigger and looking back it was all pretty basic stuff but there was no Internet back then and we took our laughs when we could get them. Anyway one day Miss Higgins was off sick and we had a supply teacher. I don't recall her name but she was a strict red faced woman and even though she had big tits we all instantly took a dislike to her. My class was just one up from the real dipshits and when it became clear that we were all getting geared up to work in the local factories, shops and building sites we all sat back and fucked about until we could all legally leave so this woman having the audacity to actually try and teach us something didn't go down well at all. We were throwing stuff about and ignoring her pleas to sit down and the more advanced boys were trying to get the more advanced girls to show a bit of bra or lift up there skirts above their leg warmers and this and that kind of carry on but Steve was doing what he did best and that was to bring someone to their fucking knees. By now I hope you can see what an asset Steve was to our mindless existence at school and on this particular day he excelled himself. Steven was an exceptional mimic and as this poor woman got more and more agitated Steven was copying her every move as he repeated what she was saying and as a confirmed anarchist I was absolutely loving the mayhem and this woman's imminent breakdown.

As she was trying to control the class she kept looking at Steven but not saying anything to him she was getting really fucking mad but having absolutely no effect until finally she slammed both her hands down onto her desk and shouted, 'the next person to make a sound will go straight to the headmaster and get a detention after school for a week! Silence. We all looked at her bulging eyes and puce cheeks. A standoff. For a minute I knew that she thought she had us ... but she didn't fucking know us.

When I was in India back in the nineties I'd been there for about a month or so and thought somehow that by then my immune system must be up and running to such an extent that it would be fine to drink water from a barrel. -I was very stoned at the time and when you're stoned you think many bad things are a good idea. When I hear folks bang on about one world governments and the queen being a shape shifting reptilian and all those other conspiracies I often think to myself that whoever believes any of it must enjoy a spliff or just be mental - anyway after a day or so after I'd done my habitual morning number two I glanced down to check on my digestive health only to find to my horror that my poop was full of worms. I was a young man back then and didn't have a care in the world and also thought I was invincible so after the initial shock I put it to the back of my mind. The next time I looked I was worm free and got on with smoking as much weed as I could get down me while travelling around India grinning like a twat and trying my best to be as spiritual as I could be without putting in any effort or knowing exactly what that meant. After my return to England I started to dwell on that incident and convinced myself that I had a tape worm growing inside me. I was always hungry and never put on any weight and any stomach upsets I got I put down to 'Rory' which was the name I'd given it. It got to the stage that when I ate anything I'd ask myself, 'what would Rory like?' I was still smoking a lot of weed and resigned myself to Rory always being inside me until he got so big he'd burst out of my chest like that thing in Alien. There was no Internet back then so I couldn't just google how to get rid of a tape worm. So I just got on with it. Then one day I was telling this story to a mate of mine and he said that you had to starve it out. So long story short I didn't eat anything for three days after which I sat naked on the floor with a saucer of milk either at the entrance of my mouth or next to my bum hole to try to temp Rory out. The idea being that as Rory was also hungry he'd smell the milk, pop his head out for a drink and I'd grab it and pull the fucker out of my body and slam it against the wall. My mate wasn't sure which end it would come out so I alternated. Anyway long story short after about a week of this it was pretty clear to me that this wasn't working so I just left it. Still to this day I wonder if Rory is still inside me or indeed if he ever was and every now and then I try to mentally prepare myself for his exit. Once I did crap out a lump of a white meaty substance but it didn't have a head and I'd been eating a lot of hake that week. I'm not sure if any of this helps but personally having learned my lesson I'd never drink out of a bathroom tap.

When I was a kid each village had its own youth club. Ours was utter shit but it was all there was so we made the best of it. We had one record player and about five records. My favourite was a rock and roll 45 called jungle rock. I could listen to it over and over and never get bored of it which was lucky because we only had the five. It's still a tune although I've just realised that I haven't listened to it for about thirty odd years so when I'm done here I'm going on the YouTube and find it and listen to it and maybe even try to do the bop. I was fucking ace at doing the bop even though I do say so myself. I was a rock n roller at heart due to all my mum's old records but I was also an indie so when I did the bop I had to do it with a sort of ironic attitude. We also had rock around the clock and the start of that tune still makes me want to rebel against something although I've put a bit of timber on since those days so not turning off lights as I leave a room or not thoroughly washing up a yoghurt pot before putting it in the recycling is about as rebellious as I get these days.

I'm happy to watch younger people having a go but for me those days are long gone. The other 45 we had was Adam and the ants. Adamant fuck me I was about thirty before I worked

29

that one out and to be honest someone dropped it into the conversation and my jaw dropped. A new royal family we want nobility fuck me two drum kits what a tune. Everyone thought he was a twat at melody maker so I had to pretend I thought he was shit but he's a legend especially when his head popped and he threw a starter motor through a pub window years after his 15 minutes were up. So yeah Steve never ever went to our youth club it was held on a Friday night so maybe it clashed with milking his beloved cows fuck knows but I never went one single time. I must have been a real prick or something because the older kids who must have been around 18 or so who ran the place kept putting the age that you could stay past nine o'clock up and up at first it was 11 then 12 then 13 the stupid wankers me and my mates would have to hang around outside and then try and sneak in but we always hit told to fuck off but anyway eventually we were allowed to stay even though there was fuck all to do but listen to those five donated records and wait for your turn to play table tennis. For some reason I was brilliant at table tennis and became definitely top three out of all us kids I still like a game to this day. The last time I played was a couple of years ago in Turkey. I'd managed to get rid of the kids by hooking them up with another couples who were about the same age and it was a master stroke but the downside was that this couple wanted to hang around with us and all I wanted to do was hang around with my wife anyway the man part of the couple turned out to be a policeman and when he told me I couldn't hide my delight. I'm joking what I actually did was inadvertently take a step back and look fucking horrified. I've never been comfortable around authority figures which I've always put down to my dad not being around much although I've no evidence for this I think I just don't like people telling me what to do but anyway this copper wasn't too bad really although he was forever grassing on my kids and every morning he'd tell me what they'd been up to the night before and I made a point of not telling my wife or giving a fuck. Anyway me and Dickson of dock green got pissed one afternoon and decided to have a game of pissed table tennis. He wasn't too bad to be fair but I held my own and eventually I beat the fucker good and proper so the next day rather than trying to persuade my wife to swerve them like I did every day I marched over to them and challenged him to another match. Well I'm a working class lad who was brought up on a building site and what we do is rip the fuck out of each other to within an inch of our lives so I let him have it about the day before when I whipped his ass thinking that he'd laugh along and take the piss back but he just flew into a massive sulk and refused to play with me again. This was such good news because we no longer had to have dinner with them every night and I didn't need to have to try and avoid them during the day so that was a double win. Anyway back to the youth club let me tell you something about how shy I was as a kid my mum was such an embarrassment all I wanted to do was curl up and die so I kept my head down to such an extent that I literally could not speak to anyone who wasn't in my circle of truth because I thought that they thought that I was a wrongun like my mum who wasn't actually that wrong she was just needy and selfish with a shit and insatiable taste in men she's got many good trait it who the fuck wants to hear that?

Anyway I'd be at this youth club and I'd be dying to buy a Mars bar or a kit Kat or a coke like all the other kids who seemed to be able to do this quite easily but for me it was a big fucking brick wall that I could never climb so I just sat about like a prize prick too shy to go up to the counter and ask some teenager for some chocolate just in case they started taking the piss out of my mum or my situation. To be fair to them they never did and looking back it all seems a bit silly but for me it was the biggest deal ever at the time. Anyway one day I woke up and thought to myself that I was no longer going to live a half-life so gave myself this protective comedy armour, put it on and I've worn it ever since. We're going back to this youth club story because there's so much to say and I got distracted by disappearing up my own arse again. Oooh a Monday crowd! Looking forward to people telling me all about paragraphs and grammar and taking breaths and this being too long to read I love hearing that kind of thing

So we're really near the thrilling conclusion of whether Steve lost his virginity or not and I for one cannot wait so let's all just put this to bed once and for all. It's now the nineties and me and my sister are outside Steve's front door. He finally recognises me and becomes animated. Hey Dom bloody hell long time no see says he. This was a fact. It was a long time since we'd seen each other so I agree with him whole heartedly. Steve looks the same but older and he's already starting to look like his dad. The last time we saw each other was at my going away piss up. Everyone, except me thought I'd only be gone for a couple of weeks. As soon as my Nan died I knew I had to go away from my village and village life. Teenage life is dull for a village boy. I didn't play darts or skittles or Sunday league football as I found these pursuits boring as fuck plus I was shit at all of them. Actually me and Steve and a few other mates founded our youth football team which I think still exists to this day in fact I think one of my nephews played for them only a few years ago which was weird because he lives fucking miles away. I remember we had this idea and then got one of my mate's dad involved. He ran the grownup team so he knew his shit. First we had to get enough players which wasn't that easy in a small village but somehow we cobbled together enough for a squad then we had to do sponsored events to raise money for a kit. We had this magazine which had loads of kits in it and I swear to you it was my choice that got chosen and the reason I chose it was because the shorts were made of some kind of silky material and I thought that they were sexy as fuck and because I was shit at football I thought that at least they'd feel good against my bollocks as I ran about in the fucking cold. I think we were about 12 or 13 which is the optimal age for teenage lads to either be wanking all the time or thinking about wanking it was for us lot anyway and when they arrived I think we all just wanted to fuck off home, put the kit on and start heating off like caged chimps. That's what I did anyway. Actually someone remind me to have a search on the google and see if I can find a pair but in a much bigger size ... 'sexy teenage boy shorts' should do the job and not get me into any trouble with the old paedo hunters at all. I'll get a pair for the wife too then we can do a bit of role play where I'm me and she's Steve ... what's that Steven you're desperate to lose your virginity and you don't care who with anymore? Well let's get you into those little shorts then sunshine because today is your lucky day! Fuck me I was miles away then. So yeah anyway we signed up to the local league and we were fucking awful and then one of the farmer's sons invited a load of his townie mates to join and we became a lot better due to the fact that there were hardly any of the original cast members left then when one of my mum's fucking boyfriends actually became our manager, I know right!? The prick. I had to fuck off too because well fuck that. I didn't even manage to steal a pair of wanking shorts before I left either. I do remember us winning something or other once because I had a little plastic trophy in my bedroom for a bit. Kid playing with constant hard-on award maybe. We also used to play youth club five aside with other villages too I now recall. Once we were playing five aside hockey and this girl from the next village who was regarded as being hot as fuck accidentally clouted me around the head with her plastic hockey stick which I took as flirtation but it transpired that it wasn't which was fine because I didn't even fancy her which was lucky for me because if I did I would have pulled her and ended up marrying her and having kids and being stuck in that village for life. Probably. Girls at my age at the time went for much older boys anyway but if a boy fancied a girl even three weeks younger than him he'd be called a fucking pervert that was the law. I think she's divorced with grandkids now like pretty much everyone I knew from back then. Except this one couple I know who married at 18 and our still together oh yeah and Steve I know exactly what his status is but now is not the time or the place to tell you all what that status is because... we'll just because I know and you don't. I could have pulled her if I wanted to you have to believe that. But I didn't want to because I had my sexy football shorts and they were more than enough at the time.

So me and Steve are up in the barn and I'm plaiting his hair while we're chatting away about boy bands and whether we should get into the new romantic phase. Steve is still into the Wurzels and finding it hard to cross over. 'I'm old school Dom' says he. I like a drummer a lead guitar a bass guitar and a lead singer and hay bales, it's as simple as that. Plus I don't have the hair for that fashion. I said 'baby doll you've got to move with the times, have you seen the lead singer from the group with the hot lead singer? What a hunk. I'm as straight as the come but that lad is to die for. Then we giggled and had a pillow fight in our nighties. What about that other group with the guy who puts flowers down his jeans I say. They're a guitar band. Nah I've heard them and not once do they mention cider or tractors it's communist propaganda and this milker is not for turning.

We were all scared shitless during the eighties because of the commies. We didn't want to have to queue round the block for a loaf of bread or pay 100 quid for a pair of dark web Levi 501s. Russia and the Eastern block were the enemy and the threat of a nuclear attack was forever imminent. Yeah their birds had high cheek bones and long legs but they were cold hearted would be assassins so we had to be vigilant. We looked to America that was the land of the brave and the free. Those mother fuckers had it all. Big cars and big houses and shit loads of money and all the latest gadgets. They had a thousand flavours of chewing gum and sky scrapers and that guy who jumped over the Grand Canyon and the bad guy who got shot by the girl in that TV series about people from Dallas and the bird with the little shorts who had two brothers who were always in trouble with the law especially the fat guy and the other guy who was his deputy and their president used to be a Hollywood actor. The Russians had fuck all except snow and female athletes who looked like fellas so they could fuck right off. Plus their music was shit. They did have some guy who invented Rubik's cube but nobody even knew his name. There was always that one kid who could do it in under a minute but they were always odd and just got them beaten up even more. I had one once it was quite therapeutic twisting and turning the fucking thing around every now and then but in the end it just reminded me of the futility of life so I smashed the fuck out of it one day. A proper Walkman was about 100 quid back then and well out of my range but I did get one that cost around a tenner and even though it was shit it was still a magical moment putting on the headphones and listening to a cassette through it. Absolutely magical. All those different sounds that I'd never heard before. Fuck knows what the first album I listened to was but I know it sounded ace as fuck. I've still got loads of cassettes somewhere I hear they're trendy again but for me they're little memories and I'll never part with them. I used to live to go into town on a Saturday and spend hours going around all the record shops and coming home with at least one cassette tape and playing it over and over and over until it was deep in my bones. One don't get time for that anymore I can't bear waiting three minutes for a YouTube advert to finish these days it's criminal really. I will put on an album and have a dance with the missus though. I can't remember whether I ever got around to finishing telling you all about Steve and his virginity or not but unfortunately we've sadly, once again, run out of Internet ink. I'm off to change the cartridge and then I'll continue the storey a bit later. Oh yeah and they had that woman who was bionic ... smash. 😊 👍 Absolutely no mention of celebrities in this post by the way not a single one just a snippet of eighties life growing up as an accidental country boy. 😊 👍

So me and Steven are sat in the bath on a typical Sunday evening listening to the top forty and chatting about robin cousin's gold medal at the Winter Olympics and the steel workers strike when I take the opportunity to ask him about his love life. Steven replied, Dom it's 1980 babe I'm still just a child and how the fuck did you get in here? I chuckle and try to change the subject. I say Steve this isn't actually happening you mad fucker you're just a conduit for my mad ramblings. This calmed him a bit but I could tell he was still unnerved especially as I started washing his hair with his little bottle of Matey. Never mind about that Steve just relax ... that Maggie Thatcher certainly divides opinion now doesn't she? I can do my own back thank you very much Steven replies. Steve is playing hard to get so i veer the topic of conversation to his favourite subject. Steven I say, if you absolutely had to, which one of all the cows you milk would you bang? You know to save the whales or them Ethiopians or such and such? Number 135 without a shadow of a mother fucking doubt bro replies Steve with a wistful look in his eye and something stirs under the bubbles. Now it was my turn to feel uncomfortable and not just because I had the tap end. Why don't you write to Jimmy Savile and ask him if he could fix it for you? I ask. I would but I can't find a pen he replies nonchalantly and we quickly change the subject once more. I said, Steven, let's burn our bras, join CND and hitchhike up to Greenham Common and try and take down the ruddy government but Steve said that he had to be sticker up for his dad's skittles team later that night and then asked why I was wearing one of his mum's bras. I said Steve, I think I might be trans and he said what's that mean and I said I'm a girl trapped in the body of a boy trapped in the body of a girl who's trapped in the body of two lads from Taunton I'm like a Russian doll but a lot thinner and wearing less gaudy makeup. Steven looked at me quizzically and then his brows furrowed and knowing he was a biter I slowly pulled myself up and off, made my excuses and left him to it. I was wearing his mother's bridal gown which made my exit rather unladylike although it did cling to me and become translucent and Steven promised to keep in touch but not with me which was all I'd ever dreamed of.

I slipped out of my dress and made my way down stairs to the living room where Steven's parents were watching bullseye. Mullets and moustaches were the order of the day and the men looked even more ridiculous if I were being honest. All the contestants were from the midlands and looked like members of the provisional IRA. Jim Bowen was on form and threw out a few sexist gags and all the old grannies in the audience pissed themselves laughing. The crafty cockney threw a ton for the chosen charity which was whippets against the bomb and Bob added thirty quid to it and counted it out during the break two sex offenders won nearly forty five quid which they gambled and lost.

They looked to see what they could have won. A speed boat but they assured Jim that they'd still had a good day and then fucked off back to the north of England to be unemployed for the rest of their working lives. Steven's parents looked at me and said, Dom we are only extras in your story and thus do not have any lines of any depth so I fucked off after making myself some angel delight and camp coffee.

I walked out into the street which had ample parking and took a piss up against the back wheel of my Ford escort mark three which is apparently perfectly legal or an urban myth anyway it was the first front wheel drive family sized car on the market and the future looked bright as fuck. Then the bloody Arggies invaded the ruddy Falklands and because Maggie Thatcher was becoming ever more unpopular the shit was about to hit the fan.

So I knock on His door and eventually he answers it and he looks at me and my sister like we were there to sell the fucker a moody carpet out the back of a van or start banging on about our lord and saviour Mr Jesus H Christ. Admittedly it had been a good few years and the last time he saw me I had a full head full of beautiful black hair and my sister had spat out at least two kids but you'd still give her one. The cheeky bastard. I said, Steven you absolute lunatic it's me Dom! He himself didn't look any different. When you don't follow fashion you don't change that much I guess. He always looked like his mum cut his hair and it always looked like a cross between David Gower and a sheep with challenging behaviour. He would have been ripe for one of those TV makeovers. Gok Wan would have had his work cut out with ole Steven though and not just because he was a biter.

The farming community don't age well to be fair. All that sun and rain and wind and cow shit takes its toll if you're adverse to moisturiser and giving a fuck about your appearance. If you've ever been to a farmer's gaff you'll know that the primary smell is cow shit. I think it must be like having a dog as in if you're not proper diligent with the Febreeze your house fucking stinks and nobody is going to tell you unless it's one of those, people don't like me because I call a spade a spade type of wankers and who'd have that lot over for tea? No mother fucker is who. When I was a kid I used to call dinner, tea. But somehow I got middle classed and now dinner is around six or seven when it used to be around 12 to one and now dinner is lunch I don't even think about it anymore. The other day I was out shopping and thought to myself, I must remember to get a couple of mangos and some cracked pepper. I didn't even blush with embarrassment. This is someone who didn't eat pasta until my Nan was long dead. Chilli con fucking what? Do I look Mexican to you? I was eighteen at least before I went to a restaurant and even then that restaurant was called MacDonald's. That's the absolute truth. I went in with a mate and had to wing it because I didn't know what the fuck was going on and just ordered what he did and just styled it out. Like sky TV, fast food was regarded as chavvy as fuck back then and if you saw a house with a satellite dish on it you knew that inside that house was members of the working class. Same with tattoos. You saw tattoos on an arm you didn't ask who the tattooist was and then start following the fuckers on Instagram you moved all your gear and fucked off in the other direction. All the hard nuts round my way went to the same tattoo artist because he was the only one there was and he was shit. All my mates from town would get to 16 or 17 and start getting awful tattoos. Plus you could go in pissed out of your head and no questions would be asked. I always wanted a Daffy Duck tattoo because along with Bugs bunny he was my hero because he was bat shit crazy and didn't give one flying fuck. Plus when he dressed up as a lady he was quite hot for a duck. Same as bugs. I'm not sure if I ever banged one out over bugs bunny dressed up as a hot dolly bird but I definitely did over Penelope Pittstop. Those legs and that waist. The dirty trollop knew exactly what she was doing. And the blonde one out of Scooby Do ... and the two birds that used to hang around with captain cave man... and Hong Kong Phooey's receptionist/

telephone operator. Fuck me no wonder my homework never got done.

So I knock on Steve's door and wait excitedly on the doorstep with my sister. I hadn't seen him for a good couple of years so couldn't wait for him to jump into my arms and embrace me like an old friend. Steve was still living in the house in which he grew up but his parents have moved up the road into his grandparent's old house or something or other I can't really remember the details. I can still recall his address which isn't like me at all but it's etched into my memory because when we were kids and fucking about playing knock and run we'd all shout out each other's names and addresses as we ran away. Steve wasn't even there most of the time so he was usually the fall guy.

Until I was old enough to get pissed I don't ever remember being bored living in a village as there was always loads to do. Especially if you had a dog, which we did. Tonic was my dog's name. Apparently there was two born at the same time so one was called gin and my dog, who was a girl dog, was called Tonic. She was a cross breed but back then we called them mongrels. She was an odd looking thing and I never did find out which two breeds of dogs shagged and made her but she looked a bit like a collie with learning difficulties. Me and my Nan inherited her from my sisters. They lived up the road with my mum and my mum's various husbands and boyfriends. Jesus I've got loads of dark stories about my mum's shit taste in men but this is about Steve and whether or not he ever lost his cherry so I'll save that for another time.

I will tell you about one of them though let's call the prick Dave although that's not his real name much like Steve I've had to change the names in order to protect people's identities like they do in films even though I couldn't care less about that but it's all a bit more intriguing and sexy if I do. So Dave turned up one day and to be fair he was a bit of a maverick and a good looking mother fucker but he was also an alcoholic. My mum spent a good amount of time in various nut houses when I was a kid and when she came out she was invariably accompanied by a new beau so they were always fucked in the head in some way or other. My mum craved attention and was forever overdosing on pills and attempting suicide especially for some reason around Christmas time when the focus should have been on the baby Jesus and Father Christmas but she wasn't having any of that shit so timed her death defying theatrics to coincide with any birthdays or Christian celebrations so that she didn't get overlooked. I don't know why I'm such a non-believer in God because as a kid a spent a lot of my time praying to the big man upstairs to let my mum live and to be fair to the lad she's still here so who the fuck am I not to believe in him. We didn't know it was all bullshit at the time although my Nan did because she'd seen it all many, many times before. I wished she'd taken us aside and said, 'look guys your mum is full of shit and she isn't going nowhere any time soon she just enjoys the limelight so fucking calm your tits. Now then who wants some angel delight?'

But she didn't so we spend our childhoods a fucking knife edge. Oh yeah Dave who's not really called Dave; actually fuck it his name was Gordon which might have been the reason he fucking drank so much. Ooh it's a boy! Let's call him Gordon! It's like calling a working class kid Piers or Boris you might as well have punched the fucker in the face at the christening just to get the poor sod used to it. Gordon is a moron. That was a tune back then and I still love it to this day but my mum was always telling us not to sing it while he was around which only made us want to sing it more. Anyway Gordon used to be a good laugh sometimes and he'd be forever bringing animals back to my mum and sister's house all sorts of strays and they'd be loved for a bit then when my sisters got bored they'd bring them down to my nan's and then we'd be lumbered with them. These days pets need to be chipped and have loads of shots and they cost a fucking fortune but back then something would get pregnant and then give birth and anyone who wanted one could have whatever came out for free usually and when it got ill it went to the vets once and never came back. Nobody paid three grand for a cat to have its appendix out it just wasn't there the next day and no questions were asked. The ones that lasted the longest were tonic my dog and puff-puff and Specko the latter two being our cats. Fuck knows what happened to puff-puff in the end. I didn't have any say in naming anything by the way Jesus I was regarded as being camp enough. Puff- puff for fuck's sake. Specko was hard as fuck though and a prolific fighter and womaniser. He scared the shit out of all the local dogs and they wouldn't come into our house with their owners unless they knew he was out. I cried like a baby the day he got run over and I saw one of my sister's friends carrying him up the path. My Nan buried him in our back garden and about six months later while I was out digging it I came across his half decomposed corpse. The shock of that experience I'll never forget and it actually felt like his soul entered me and it was terrifying although since then I've been an absolute whizz at climbing trees and licking my own arse hole.

So Steve is now spending all his milk money flying off to Indonesia in an attempt to find love. The trouble with the next part of this saga is pretty much everything from here on in is second hand information. I know the result of these excursions but I can't tell you with any real certainty what happened in between him telling me he'd fallen for some girl who worked in a hotel to the next time I saw him when I turned up at his door years later. I hadn't seen the fucker for a good few years before me and one of my sisters rang his bell on a whim when we went to put flowers on my Nan's grave.

I've always liked churches and cemeteries; I find them calming. During the day anyway. During the night they seem to be full of drunken goths or couples shagging but on a sunny, crisp spring morning I've always found them to be pleasant places. Typically I will stand at my Nan's grave and tell her things that have happened to me since the last time I visited. I do this but I don't think that this is where her spirit hangs out. When I die if I've got a choice I'll be hanging around the Brazilian national women's volleyball team's changing rooms. I've given this a lot of thought. This is assuming that you can still knock one out in the afterlife. If not I'll just sit on a cloud and get stoned and watch people going about their business. I'd pour myself a cup of filtered coffee - if it's heaven then obviously nobody will be drinking instant coffee because if they do I'll be asking for my money back. What's that you say Saint Steve no coffee or weed up here? I thought this was paradise? Open the gates mother fucker because I'm out. Then I'll slap on some factor fifty, press the down button and take my chances with old Louie Cipher.

I love watching people and giving them a back story. I could write a good sized novel on every single person I've ever met or even seen. Even the dull looking ones. Ordinary lives are fascinating especially old people's. If I meet someone who is old and they've still got a glint in their eye then I want to know how they've managed it. I've been a decorator since the eighties and I've always loved it because with a job like mine you have the freedom to day dream and you meet people from all walks of life. I've been in thousands of houses and it's still a thrill to knock on a client's door not knowing who's on the other side. Council estates are the best because there's always a lot going on. If you're a single teenage boy working on a council estate it's like being in a sweet shop. A sweet shop full of sexually frustrated women. Of course your middle class cis female will put out too as will the upper classes but on a council estate nobody is beating around the bush. Fuck knows why there has never been a carry on up the council estate or confessions of a painter and decorator because I for one would watch that with one hand in my pocket. One thing I know for sure is that everyone likes a bit of rough and if you're wearing a pair of overalls you can get away with murder. Apart from that wicked beastliness you also make a lot of friends.

Too many friends really. If I work in somebody's house for a week or so I'm friends with the whole family. Once people realise that you're not going to rob them or shit everywhere and that in fact you are totally normal the guards come down and suddenly you're part of the family. I've baby sat kids and walked dogs and sat listening to people telling me their most intimate secrets and fears and at the end of the job exchanged numbers and we've all promised to meet up again and go for drinks but nine times out of ten once I'm back in the car that's the end of it. One can't have thousands of friends because that's just impossible. It's like when you meet people on holiday and promise to keep in touch, it's not going to happen. Oh yeah Steve and his holiday romance! Oh well we're nearly there now but once again I seemed to have gone off topic so you'll just have to wait a bit longer. It'll be worth it I promise even though we know my promises are pretty much worthless. I'm off for a coffee. I miss people watching and crowds. I love coffee and crowds. You wait until I get to tell you about when I went to India duck me I've got some great stories about that country. Jesus I'm old now. They say time goes faster as you get older but I feel like I've been around for ages and as I plan to live until at least 150 some of you lot may never find out what the fuck every happened to Him and his cheery. You mother fuckers had best put out those fags, cut back on saturated fat and sugar and start exercising if you want to see this out. Forgive any typos because I'm not going to go back over all that lot now.

Back in the eighties you only had the four TV channels which meant that when you went to school all your mates would have watched the same thing as you. My mates watched the young ones and if you didn't watch the young ones you were a massive twat because the young ones sorted the men from the boys. If you remember the kid that burnt himself to a crisp in Spain and liked Steve Davis over Alex Higgins then you won't be surprised to know that he didn't like the young ones. Fuck knows why we let him hang around with us to be honest. Steve didn't watch the young ones either but I think that was either because it clashed with his beloved cows getting their tits sucked out or he just watched what his mum and dad watched. He loved his mum and dad and enjoyed their company which I found odd because my mum was a complete embarrassment to me with all her boyfriends and husbands and I didn't really want that much to do with her at the time. Once I was playing in my nan's garden - as I said before, my Nan brought me up- my mum came up to me and said, just to let you know Dom, I got married yesterday. I didn't even reply. Bad parents can really fuck up a child's childhood but I had my Nan and even though she wasn't the most demonstrative or tactile of people I knew she loved me and that was good enough for me. Sometimes a boy needs a bear hug though and not getting one burns. I'm a hugger I'll hug anyone as long as it's consensual. We weren't hugged as kids though. I don't think anyone was back then. I don't think hugging was the done thing for members of the working class. Even today if I hug my dad I can feel him tense up and it's sad but there you go. My sisters don't really hug either it's learned behaviour but I broke that mould and pre bat flu I nominated myself as the family hugger whether anyone liked it or not. Now all our kids are huggers and I put that down to me.

One of my sisters had a friend called Claire - this was only about 15 or so years ago- their kids used to go to the same Catholic school as we did as kids anyway this Clair was a big woman- we used to call big people fat people back then- rude as fuck really, but anyway the first time we met at some Catholic associated function or other I instinctively gave her a hug and she hugged me back and it was fucking amazing. It was like going back into the womb and I felt all warm and safe and cosy. Me and her loved to have a hug. Even 15 years ago I was still extremely beautiful as you can no doubt imagine so she probably got some kind of sexual thrill from it and I couldn't blame her but for me it was like taking medicine and felt rejuvenated afterwards. We'd always seek each other out for a hug and that was usually the highlight of the day. Actually the best bit of one of those Catholic days out was when the priest used to come back to one of my sisters' houses because everyone was shit scared of him. Not me though because I was a non-believer and my job was just to make sure he didn't get any opportunities to fiddle any of the kids. For me he was just a dubious man in a frock. One time we were all sitting around in one of my sister's living rooms and you could cut the tension with a knife so because I'm a nice guy I decided to break the ice. Someone told me that this twat was an Arsenal fan so I looked up and gleefully said, hey father, someone told me that you're a massive gooner! Everyone shat themselves and it became clear that nobody but me and the priest knew what this meant. From their point of view I might as well have said, hey father somebody told me that you were a massive homosexual. This was their mistake not mine and I just sat there all innocent until he eventually started banging on about football and everyone relaxed. I didn't mind going to church as an adult though because you knew that sooner or later you could get pissed. I only ever went to confession once and it was shit. It wasn't like in films where you go into that box and the priest is on the other side and it's all a bit dark and sexy mine was fave to face sat in a hall on one of those little chairs. Fucked if I was going to tell that prick any of my juicy stories so I made a few things up and he gave me ten Hail Marys, told me to do four star jumps in my pants and vest and then wanked me off. Well fuck me that was even more rambling than usual but last time I got a post deleted for mentioning Gilbert and George and now I'm on post approval so I didn't want to get too deep into Neil and Vivian and Rick and the rest of those young ones although I will say that we all identified with the different characters and did our impressions of them. Brian Damage was my favourite because he was the most mental. I remember Steve doing admirable impressions of all of them even though he'd never seen it he just copied ours. The lad had a lot of talent to be fair.

Spoiler alert. Tonight I'm going to tell you whether Steve ever did get laid. But first I'm going to tell you how I saved his life. At the back of his house was a field and for some reason me and another mate and Steve were hanging out in it. Fuck knows why though because when we were primary school kids me and Steve didn't really hang out that much because I didn't go to their poxy village school so for some reason he was suspicious of me. Anyway there was some kind of storm drain in the field - I say storm drain I don't have a clue what it was - but it had two concrete blocks on the top with little metal handles embedded into them. Even at the time I wondered why there could be a storm drain in the middle of a field. It was mental. I don't know one thing about farming and fields although cows are great especially calves.

Calves are loads of fun and always jolly and happy then you look round and they are cows and they've gone mad. If you've ever been chased by a herd of cows you'll know what fun it is because it's like a game to them and you know that if they caught you they wouldn't do fuck all. They'd be all like, ha ha ha we chased you, and we'd be all like, I know right!? And then they'd gather around at a safe distance and stare at you with their big mad eyes and sooner or later one would jump up on another ones back and put on a bit of cumbersome lesbian sex show. It's less sexy than it sounds because cows are mental and not at all attractive. Apart from this one cow ... but anyways... I do know that each one has a personality though and when they go to get milked there's always a pecking order. Fuck me I must have spent more time on the farm than I thought. Oh yeah it was because they had a snooker table in a barn and we were allowed to play on it. We took snooker very seriously for a while. We all had our own cues although some where better than others. Me and my best mate had proper cheap ones because we were poor and obviously Steve had one that cost ten million quid which was a lot of money back then. I think my highest break was 36 there wasn't any YouTube tutorials to study at the time and I remember buying a book on how to play better snooker. I think Ray Reardon wrote it because it was dull as fuck but I did learn that you don't just whack fuck out of the cue ball and hope for the best. You could tell someone's personality by which snooker player they preferred. I loved Alex Higgins because his snooker was thrilling and full of passion and emotion and he was unpredictable I loved that he was pissed all the time. So if someone said they preferred him to Steve Davis then I knew

I'd like them. I had a mate who preferred Steve Davis and we used to argue as to why we thought our favourite was the best and how the other one was a prick. Actually he was the kid who went on holiday with us and barbecued himself in the searing Spanish sun and had to walk around in little plastic feet bags so I rest my case. That doctor was hot though. She looked like female Doctors do in porn films. Think of Barbara Windsor in carry on Doctor but replace her face with Penelope Cruz and completely change what she was wearing and then add doctor Martin shoes and bare legs and she had big brown eyes like my favourite cow. I didn't really have a favourite cow obviously but a couple of the other kids did which is deep village shit. cows don't have names though they just had numbers so they'd say that 143 was their favourite or 235 which wasn't at all fucked up. There were rumours that some kids used to stick their dicks in them but I never witnessed anything like that ... but if you knew some of these fuckers you wouldn't be that surprised if it was true. Imagine if when you were a teenager you actually shagged a cow for real. I don't think I could live with myself. I'm sure it happens but thank fuck I never found bestiality sexy.

I loved that this Spanish Doc was laughing at my mate's predicament too but not in a horrible way like we all were and I liked the bit where his lip started going and my mate went, don't cry mate and if this hot doctor hadn't been there he would have burst into tears. I hope teenage boys are as cruel to each other as we were you just had to soak it up and it was ace. Even today if I was out with my mates all we'd want do so is take the piss out of each other and hope someone really fucks up somehow so we can never let them forget it. Ever. So me and Steve and another mate stumbled across this drain thing and decided to have a look inside. The concrete covers were well heavy but we managed to move one and we saw that it went down about two metres or something I think there was a ladder that you could climb down too but I'm not a hundred percent so Steve is pushing the second concrete cover so we can get into it but because he's a soppy twat he's ended up pushing down into the drain and his fingers get trapped in the handles so he starts to fall with it. I can see him now halfway down that drain freaking the fuck out and I remember looking at this spectacle and thinking, fuck me he's wearing some expensive jeans, the spoiled little dick head. Eventually, like a hero, I managed to grab hold of the concrete block and lift it back out without breaking Steve's fingers. He didn't say thank you because as I said, the lad was twisted but his dad must have heard his screams because he came running over and bollocked him for fucking about. I think Steve's dad was the only person in the world that he was scared off. His dad didn't bollock us though because he knew my Nan and if he'd fucked with me my Nan would have bollocked him because she was a fucking force of nature. Oh heck I haven't told you whether Steve ever got laid and now it's too late.

Don't trust me. I can't be trusted.

Anyway as Jimmy Krankie once told the Dali lama ... 'it's not the destination it's the journey now then are you going to eat that last bit of soya protein or fucking what bruv?'

Steve didn't like hot drinks. Not tea or coffee or hot chocolate or anything hot. I found this to be very odd. We were all big tea drinkers in our house. Tea was the common denominator. I lived with my Nan as you all know by now and she was like the matriarch in our close and the place was chock a block with neighbours coming and going. Knock and enter was the protocol.

Nobody knocked and waited they all just tapped and came in through the back door. Only official people knocked on our front door. Well the butcher and baker did actually and the rent man. And during the turbulent years the police but that was always to do with my mum and whichever step dad or boyfriend was causing trouble at the time.

Oh yeah and the gypsies used to knock on our door and ask if we needed any knives sharpened and the carpet guy used to come in I didn't trust that fucker he'd always try and buy my nan's big clock for five quid the cheeky bastard.

All our neighbours used the back door. Snigger. One neighbour was called George he was old and he'd come round every day for a cup of tea and he'd cry because he missed his wife who had died years earlier I adored him he had white hair and he always used to say it was because he washed it with

Persil and I believed him. I used to put his eye drops in for him because I was the only one he could trust. Please don't make nonce quips about him because I'll block you.

Another neighbour used to come around during the day off her nut with a carrier bag full of empty whiskey bottles that she would put in our bin because she didn't want her husband to know she was an alcoholic. He did know though. Another neighbour would come round in tears because her husband was shagging someone else. Another would come round and just sit with my Nan because she 'suffered with her nerves' she was anorexic too. I could make her laugh her fucking head off though. I think I've always felt obliged to cheer people up if that's what they need and still do this at every given opportunity, anyway they'd all come round and drink tea and have a moan up and my Nan would sit and listen with a cigarette hanging out of her mouth, the smoke rising up and giving her grey hair a ginger streak, and she'd just let them get on with it and keep all their secrets. My Nan's husband died building that bridge over the river Kwai so I never met him. She never talked about him so I never asked and the only time I saw her show any emotion was on Armistice Day when she'd break her heart.

I still drink a lot of tea but coffee is my go to these days I reckon I was about twenty before I drank 'real' coffee though before that it was always instant I didn't even know there was a choice up until I went to France and they were all drinking filtered coffee.

I can't drink instant coffee these days though because I'm a coffee snob. It's my only vice these days apart from heroin. Steve still doesn't drink hot drinks to this day. I still find that fucked up. You ever gone into someone's house and they offer you a drink and say that they don't have coffee or tea because they don't like it themselves and you think, you cheeky bastard I'll just have tap water then. Because I don't.

I've just realised that I have no idea what Steve's mum and dad did for a living which is odd because as a village boy you know everything there is to know about everyone.

I know they had a good standard of living though because they had a car. We didn't have a car which was inconvenient as fuck when I look back. If you have to rely on the two bus services that went through the village your freedom is severely curtailed. As I said previously I went to school 6 miles away so most my friends lived in town so any birthday parties were out of the question. I didn't even mention any invitations to my

Nan so that she wouldn't get embarrassed because we couldn't afford a taxi.

I remember being invited to one once and because I couldn't go his mum made me a little bag of sweets and cakes and probably a little toy or whatever I say probably because I never got to see it. Well I saw the little bag when I was presented with it by a teacher who told me to keep it in my school bag until after school I was only about eight or nine at the time so I did as I was told. We kept all our bags in a communal cloakroom and when I went to get it at break the prick whose birthday it was had nicked it and ate it. His name was Simon I wish I could remember his last name because it still burns me that I didn't kick his head in.

Before I could react a teacher came in and gave him a proper bollocking and then handed me a couple of screwed up plastic soldiers which I put in the bin. He left soon after so I didn't get my revenge.

That's another thing you miss when you don't have a dad around because if my son came home and told me that this had happened to him then I would have gone to their house and flayed the perp in front of his parents and then killed their dog. In all my primary school life I only ever went to one party and that was because it was the birthday of my best friend Serge. He was a French kid. His accent was very strong and he was a good looking lad like me and we ruled our school and had many girlfriends even if we didn't even kiss or hold hands or even talk to them that much it was more a prestige thing. When I say we ruled the school we only ruled it fleetingly in our last year because up until then we had to keep our heads down because the kids in the year above were hard as fuck. Working class Catholics are a brutal bunch especially if they're Irish. When we went to church for our communions or if my dad came down for the weekend and we were forced to go, we'd see the families of these hard kids and knew instinctively to keep the fuck away.

These families invented the neck and hand tattoos long before the middle class got hold of the idea. Back then having a tattoo meant you were a dangerous mother fucker not that you had a grand spare to cover one arm with clocks and watches and inspirational bollocks written in script. These said, mum and dad or Leeds or Bristol city or you could have a hinge on the crook of your elbow or a swallow between your thumb and index finger or, made in Somerset, written across your neck or scissors cutting along a serrated line across your throat. Or skins. Most clubs and pubs wouldn't let you in if you had tattoos back then. I remember going to see bad manners years after they had their last hit and the place was full of old skins with faded head tattoos that were now incongruous because these guys had grown up and got jobs and stopped fighting and now just looked like your average middle aged men.

Catholic school are multicultural places and the pupils come from all over the place. Black, white, brown if your family believed that the pope was the mouthpiece of God then you were welcome. If you were from another religion though you'd better keep the fuck back a bit. Especially if you were a Protestant. We've been down that road though.

Oh yeah my mate serge and his birthday party. Well I pulled up in a taxi like a king and my Nan came with me and took me to the door, introduced herself then mercifully fucked off. Now all my mates thought I had the oldest mum in the world which wasn't embarrassing as fuck at all. Serge's parents were both French and hysterically couldn't speak one word of English which was ace. I was too young to think about having a wank about his mum when I got home but I do remember that she had a nice set of bangers and wasn't wearing a bra which you could probably go to jail for these days. I remember their being loads of nice food and they had a nice stereo player with big speakers and I also remember we played statues or whatever that game is where you play music and when it stops you have to stand still. Serge's dad was in charge of this game but unfortunately for him and for us he was evidently deaf as a post because he'd turn the music down a bit then start manically pointing at us saying that we were moving, that's what we thought he said anyway because he English was so shit. We could still hear the music though so we all just looked puzzled as he tried to get us to sit down. So that was my one and only party experience. Steve didn't go to any that I was aware of though because he didn't get invited to any because no sane person would want that utter lunatic in their house.

I grew up in a village in the eighties and everyone knew everyone including everyone in all the neighbouring villages because we all went to the same shitty secondary school and drank in the same pubs - the posh kids who went to private schools and people that didn't go to the pub obviously being an exception- anyway everyone also knew who was shagging who and who was shagging someone else on the side plus there were loads of hearsay and rumours flying about in all directions. It was ace.

My family or should I say my mum was fucking scandalous back then but luckily for me my mate's mum was even worse and she'd often get spotted with some other woman's husband walking down a quiet lane hand in hand until getting spotted and jumping into hedges to hide and the like - a bit like that women from the hit BBC series, last of the summer wine- The parallels are quite uncanny to be honest. These were just rumours though and I personally never saw anything like that and I loved his mum because unlike so many other people she was always genuinely nice to me.

They say that girls mature faster than boys and I came to believe this because there was always a lot of girls my age who were shagging much older men and they'd walk about all sophisticated and that while us lads were mostly still wanking off to porkies or the village communal jazz mag. I didn't know one single teenage boy who was shagging an older woman even though that was all our ultimate fantasy and all any of us talked about. Frequently a girl would come into the pub with mascara running down her face theatrically sobbing her heart out telling anyone who would listen that she'd been dumped by this guy who was sometimes a good twenty years older than her who had a wife and kids and it never occurred to any of us that these guys were taking advantage of these girls naivety or grass the guy up and tell his unsuspecting wife. One notorious story was of a local village sword smith who had seven kids by his wife but as he was clearly mental and an alcoholic and would shag anyone who crossed his wicked path she'd eventually left him and a few weeks later he moved in his latest conquest who couldn't have been more than 17 years old and these days would have probably been classed as being on the spectrum -on the left side of it but still on it- who suddenly found herself looking after all his kids, a couple of which were older than her. To be fair to them I think they did stay together until the day he fell off a roof and died.

I'm not judging anyone here and never have and as I said at the time nobody questioned it. On the contrary we looked up to some of these guys in a way but looking back it was all a bit seedy and also involved a lot of strong cider and Ford Capris. Actually that reminds me of the time I had two pints of old school scrumpy at Glastonbury festival and went blind for about half an hour but I don't want to bore anyone with that just yet.

A couple of years ago, more or less, to be honest I don't really have any idea how long ago it was, anyway I went out into my garden and saw a baby pigeon sat on the decking. Well I'm not that good looking lad off spring watch but my instinct told me that it had obviously fallen out of its nest and was therefore vulnerable. My next instinct was to turn around and go back in and let nature take its course but then my catholic guilt kicked in like it always does on these occasions and I reluctantly decided to throw the little fucker a bone, metaphorically speaking obviously. I looked at it and it looked at me and then we formed some kind of spiritual bond or something because I suddenly developed an overwhelming urge to help it. My first act was to name it Dave. I can't tell the sex of a bird just by looking at it and there was no way I was going to start rooting around looking for genitals especially in the current climate so rightly or wrongly I assumed its gender. My next act was to go to the shed and get out the recycling box I'd taken with me from when I lived in Brighton as it had a lid and was exactly the right size for Dave to stay in until he was fit enough to fuck back off. I didn't have any hay which would have been perfect because I'm not a farmer so I ripped up an old newspaper and used that for Dave's bedding. I then went back inside and rummaged through our collection of cereals. I found Rolled oaks and cornflakes and even some flax seeds that I bought when I fantasised about getting back into shape and eating clean but then couldn't be bothered so I mixed up a little concoction and put it all on a plate. I've seen pigeons eat dog ends and sick before now so thought that would be more than good enough and plus if I do something I always try and do it right and I've always considered myself an excellent host and Dave was now my guest. Dave was either extremely brave or thick as shit because he was quite happy for me to pick him up and put him in the box. As it was getting late I put him in the shed, bid him goodnight and fucked off back indoors. The next morning full of trepidation I went to check in him and to my delight he was already up and had eaten all the food. This was good news so I took the box with Dave in it and put it outside. I then removed the lid. Obviously I hadn't put the lid on tight but at an angle so he could still breathe. Anyway Dave gave me a look and then hopped up onto the edge of the box. By now of course I loved Dave but also wanted him to fuck off but I think those flax seeds made him think that he was on holiday or something because he had no intention of leaving. For three days I fed the fucker and then tucked him up at night. On day four he jumped up on the ledge of the box, had a look around and then flew up and on to our garden fence. I'd seen his mum and dad up in the trees during our time together but they didn't really seem to be giving much of a shit if I'm being honest although they did keep looking down and cocking their heads but I think all birds to that. Anyway long story short he eventually fucked off up into the trees and settled down on a branch next to his parents. On occasion I'll see Dave and shout, Dave! And once he came when I called but to be honest it might not have been Dave at all because the three of them look identical. It's been a good while since I saved Dave's life and I'm invested in him so like this morning when I see the three of them hanging out together I can't help thinking that maybe it's time for him to find a partner and literally leave the nest but I don't know at what age a pigeon reaches sexual maturity and I've never been that arsed enough to google it. It's always nice to see the little dick head though.

Steve may have been unlucky in love but was lucky in different ways one being that his parents didn't give a shit about religion ie they were Church of England, which is definitely a 'hands off' religion unlike mine. I was a Catholic, still am I guess. I don't think you can leave once you're in. I'm happy that I've been baptised and confirmed though because I'll need all the help I can get if there actually is a God.

I lived in a village but didn't go to the village school. I had to take a bus 6 miles to the local Catholic school. This had its advantages and disadvantages. Advantages, a good solid primary school education and the food was superb. Everyone knows that the catholic schools are the best. Unless you're not a catholic and go to one. Then you're fucked. My mate used to get thrown around and kicked about just for being a Protestant by our form teacher who was a very red faced, upright, sexually frustrated nun. And not one of those sexy ones off those saucy films either. She loved me though because I was in the firm. Apparently I pulled her veil off once when I was an infant and everyone shat themselves because they all knew that she could go ape shit but she laughed her head off and after that I was untouchable. Maybe that's where my cheekiness came from. Women have mostly always found me to be charming whereas men have, in the main, found me to be annoying as fuck. I'm happy with this. I was never a fighter but if someone fucked with me then I'd have their girlfriend away at the drop of a hat. That was just a fact. I've been in many an unsavoury situation while growing up and seen more than my fair share of fights. I love a fight but I don't ever want

79

to get involved in it and everyone has always instinctively understood that. I remember one time when the whole fucking pub kicked off, it was like one of those fights from the old westerns and everyone was punching fuck out of everyone else it was absolute mayhem but I was walking about like Moses parting the waves. I could walk into a skinhead pub with a biker mate or a biker pub with a skin head mate and before it all got a tasty somebody would recognise me from the building sites and everyone would calm the fuck down because everyone knew I was a harmless clown. I was fucking beautiful back in the day though I mean it would have been a crime to have punched my exquisite boat. Sure what you see today is just another Middle Aged man indistinguishable from every other old twat, you'd bang me but only on a pill or after a good few lines now but even I would have shagged me back in the day and I have very high standards. So yeah I was a cocky little Catholic boy and at school I was very happy because the place was crawling with the little fuckers but back in the village I was the kid who lived with his Nan even though his mum lived up the road and I was a Catholic in a world of Church of Englanders and I had an Irish name. Dominic John Paul O'Neill it doesn't get anymore Irish Catholic than that unless your name is paddy Rosary O'Papist or something so if I got into any argument as a kid I'd be always called a thick Irish IRA ruddy bugger or words to that effect. Being Irish is cool as fuck these days but not in the eighties oh no. I used to get stopped at Bristol airport every single time when me and my mates used to fly off to Greece or Spain. In the end I used to step out of line with my passport out because I knew the dick in the cheap suit was going to pick me out anyway. Where are you going sir? Corfu. Business or pleasure? Who the fuck has business in Corfu apart from being one of those twats outside pubs giving away flyers that say two for one. Jesus Mary and Joseph I still sweat like Jimmy Savile outside an orphanage when I go through security. That's when you grow a thick skin and develop such a scathing sense of humour that people think twice about giving you shit. I actually look forward to it sometimes just so I can unleash it because it is a type of art in a sense. Me and Steve were good mates but he called me an Irish c*** once even then I new that he only said it because he was angry and a bit mental and also knew absolutely fuck all about Anglo Irish politics so I didn't even mind that much because I knew for certain that at the end of the day he hadn't been baptised so as much as I loved him he was going to burn in the fiery pits of hell for all eternity... but before he did he got back on that plane for a second visit to his poor little waitress crush and that's where the fun really starts. Amen brothers and sisters until next time, Sláinte.

If there's a better day to put an end to the mini saga that is my old mate Steve's love life then I don't know what that day is and even if I did I wouldn't tell you and even if I did tell you I'd tell you in a language that you wouldn't understand so it would be the same result.

A nil- nil draw at home in the rain.

But I digress, let's crack on as I know that all of you without exception will be making sweet, sweet love to your partners this morning and thus have better things to do than read my scream of consciousness ramblings. If someone had called their bird or fella their partner back in the day where I came from then whoever heard you say it would either think that you were a new age hippy or hinting that you were a homosexual.

To this day I've never been able to say it without cringing deep inside myself and that's why I got married because that opened up a whole new vocabulary for me. The wife, the missus, the old ball and chain, her in -doors (from minder that one was) talking of which as I lived with my Nan while growing up she was old school and for some reason thought ITV was the devil's work because it contained adverts so I never got to see the likes of minder or the Sweeney or Tiswas or the A team or anything cool like that but for some reason coronation street was ok. Bloody double standards if you ask me but I don't begrudge Corrie because back then I loved it. Well Hilda and Stan Ogden and Eddie and that old bird who ran the Rovers and Bet and Jack and Vera and even managed to bash one out on occasion over Gail Tilsley yeah she didn't have much of a chin but she could wear a tight pair of jeans, a very tight pair of jeans, and what she lacked in facial symmetry she more than made up for in ass. Apparently she suffered with dreadful hospitalising bouts of thrush because of those tight fitting jeans but I think we all thought that was a price worth paying. Corrie was beautifully written and camp as fuck. Gritty realism in drag and very funny. What the hell has this got to do with our Steve though? I do not know. This is about Gail now. Actually can somebody remind me to have a quick one off the wrist about her? Cheers. Oh yeah so I was home alone the other day and as I was going through all the TV channels I came across the Sweeney on ITV 8 or something so I thought I'd give it a go. What a pile of sexiest wank. Badly written homoerotica in my opinion although there was loads of giggling birds in bikinis which was a highlight. I was never allowed to watch all those bond films either which now I've seen them was a blessing in my opinion because they were shit but I've since wondered if I had seen them as a kid would I have been inspired and been an international spy by now or at least minced about in a wig churning out sexual innuendos. That miss money penny did hand me my degree though which was a highlight of the day when I graduated from east London University. The price is right. Never saw it. Bullseye. Never saw it. I tell you what though if you ever feel like laughing your head off you can do worse than getting stoned and watching repeats of Bullseye. The fashions are superb. The haircuts are to die for and Jim's chats with the contestants are pure gold. 'There's your thirty quid that's yours to keep unless you want to gamble it and try and win some fucking spoons Dave?' No? You're keeping the money and fucking off back to the midlands? Well I don't blame you for that son.' I could watch it on a loop for the rest of my life no problem.

Once I walked into my French class when I was about fourteen only to find two, yes two Valentine's cards on my desk. What a day to remember. But this isn't about me though it's about Steve and whether he ever did get laid but unfortunately I need to find a garage that's open so I can buy her indoors three quid's worth of flowers and some of those little

chocolates with the hazelnuts in them

Fuck it let's have two in a day as you're a good bunch in the main. So Steve flew off in a big iron bird to find love but this wasn't the first time he'd flown oh no. Me and Steve had been to a few far flung places together before he decided to go somewhere on his own. Hang on maybe I was holding the fucker back? I hadn't thought of that. Maybe I was such a bad wingman that girls were repelled by him!? Oh well fuck him it's too late now.

So yeah boys holidays what a lark. Especially for a load of country bumpkins like us. We turned up in Spain with opened toed wellington boots and a can do attitude. Once you tell someone that you're a West Country boy you've got a reputation to uphold. And uphold it we did. Two Sambuca's in and we were giving it, I am a cider drinker I drinks it all of the day! I am a cider drinker it soothes me troubles away oh are oh are eh oooh are oooh are eh. Fuck knows how you spell that but you get the gist. The same thing happens to us as happens to the Irish or the Welsh or the Scots as soon as you say you're a West Country lad whoever you're speaking to suddenly starts doing their impression of you. There's nothing you can do but laugh along especially if they've got big tits and a northern accent because you knew you were in. That's a sweeping statement and also that a scientific fact.

I could hold my own in any situation except one and that was if we were in a bar and they had a live band because the lead singer could always take his pick of the girls in the crowd and take their pick they did. One swooped a girl off her feet right from under my nose it was almost like sorcery. It was onwards and upwards for me though because the north is a big place especially if you include Scotland and Wales it was like shooting fish in a barrel but still Steve couldn't get his end away. I'd often come back from some fleeing tryst to find him banging on about football to some old man I an empty bar and I'd despair but at least he was out of the hotel room

one time I think it was in the Gran Canaries one of my mates got off the plane on the first day dumped his bag in the hotel and then proceeded to lay on the beach for about eight hours. He was whiter than a milk bottle when he arrived as we all were but that night he turned lobster red and hot sun stroke apparently. We didn't know this at the time we just knew he was laying on his bed with a temperature and sunburn. It was about a week before we starred to give a shit so we escorted him down to the local chemist. I remember the doctor being well hot all dark hair and big Spanish eyes and olive skin and I was thinking that if I lived here I'd be ill in my penis area all the time. It was a woman by the way although some of those Spanish men would have turned the head of even the straightest guy. Especially if they were hoisting themselves up out of the pool all wet and wearing skimpy speedos.

Nom nom...

Fuck me where was I?

Oh yeah me being sexist towards that doctor bird. God I was an even bigger wanker back then. Anyway she took one look at my mate and said he was basically fucked and dehydrated and his trotters were so badly burnt that she made him wear these little blue plastic bags on the fuckers. He was examined behind a screen and when he came out looking all sorry for himself wearing these ridiculous foot bags we all absolutely pissed ourselves to such an extent even doctor Spain joined in it was absolutely brilliant. The poor lad was nearly in tears. It was a ruthless time and rightly so. He was fine in the end and the only one to come back with any money.

Steve liked to go on trips and once while I was out of the hotel room one afternoon some fit rep had the obviously been knocking because when I got back everyone's cock was hard and they started banging on about this big party that they'd all signed up for and they'd also paid for me so it was on. This fit bird was single and was going to be there and they all convinced themselves that they were going to give her one. Sigh. So long story short we jumped on this bus around seven in the evening and after about two hours we arrived at this shitty ranch type bollocks and the only birds there were the old grannies dishing up what looked like horse and chips. That was the highlight of the night. If I wanted to drink warm beer and hang around with sunburnt Geordies I could have popped down to the local taverna and saved myself a good few quid. No sign of the fit bird either Jesus we were all so naive.

For a good week I was shouting 'taxi!' At the top of my voice like I thought everyone else was doing, until a girl from hull politely as she was able to while laughing her fucking head off told me that the correct term was actually, Aciiiid! I'm glad we were only there for two weeks because I was dying with Shame.

My eyes were opened though and I knew then that there was more to life than a village could ever give me. Oh yeah a few days later he'd convinced us to go on some fucking boat trip with an early start and we all had good intentions but on the morning everyone but Steve couldn't be arsed to go and he flew into a proper temper it was brilliant then he slammed the door and fucked off to go on his own so we all went giggling back to sleep only to see him arrive back again about half an hour later because it was too stormy what a result we even got our deposits back but Steve sulked the rest of the day. When you get five guys in one hotel room with all that hot sex to be had but it's just out of reach then that's going to cause an awful lot of teenage spirit which will always lead to teenage furtive wanking. I mean I've never been ashamed to bash one out or talk about bashing one out but not everyone is like that and it was loads of fun trying my best to spoil my other mates more clandestine bouts of self-pollution. We could be out in a pub or somewhere and one lad would say, right guys I'm just popping back to the room for a bit I won't be long... this was code for, I want to have a wank but can't if anyone is about, so I'd get another mate to come with me so it didn't just look quite as gay and then we'd follow him back to the room and quietly let ourselves in and then at the most inappropriate time bang like fuck on the door so hopefully he'd shoot his country load all over himself while at the same time shitting his self and calling us that naughty c word.

Sounds a lot more homoerotic now than it did back then but as I keep saying we didn't have the Internet so had to make up our own fun. Fuck me you've been spoiled today now ain't cha. Fuck any paragraphs they're so last year and the lack of them sorts out the wheat from the chaff 😄 👍

So even though Steve had to get on a plane he'd finally found someone to focus his cis male attention on. Or did he? Rhetorical question. It's a bloody mine field in here ain't it? Rhetorical question. I do like rules though. It burns me to follow them but for other people they're a good idea. If you post, what's everyone's favourite type of cheese? You're cheating a bit because you're dangling your hook with a big juicy worm on the end and the chances are you'll get a few more bites than if you said, I'm bored, because the latter has obeyed the rules but missed the point. The answer to the first question is obviously, knob cheese, by the way just in case it comes up. Which it won't. Not for very long anyway.

Fuck knows why I just got bogged down with that shit but hey ho it's written now and if there's one thing I don't do it's delete. Once it comes out of my brain and travels down my neck, through my arm and out of my right thumb it's here for good. I wonder how long all this Facebook malarkey will last for? Rhetorical question. Fuck me I can't wait until I'm bored of writing that but one can't be too blasé because I've learned that there's always going to be some frustrated writer sitting in the wings waiting for folks like me to slip up so they can scream, rule breaker! Drag this mother fucker out by his hair and throw him down the staircase and into the street! He's not the Messiah he's a very naughty self-reflexive cock end! Exterminate! Exterminate! As they wank themselves into an angry frenzy of sanctimonious self-loathing.

Actually I've got loads of stories about bouncers, the brutes. They're called door security now or something but back in the day we just called them wankers. I must admit that some of the female ones did open up a kink in me but I'm a face man and call me old fashioned but my only rule was that I'd never date anyone with a stronger jawline than me or have bigger bollocks.

Twenty minutes covered in baby oil and wrestling with one or ten of these Amazonian goddesses would have worked for me though. Actually will somebody remind me that when I'm on my last legs I want a - I wonder what the collective noun is for a gang of female door birds full of steroids but I will never ask that question in here- anyway I want them to all dress up like the fit one off gladiators ... Wolf I think his name was... joking her name was Jet she's etched in my mind forever because I spent a lot of my youth fantasising about whipping off all that Lyra and giving her one while shouting Aroooooga!

Anyway yeah I'd like a bunch of them to kick me to death while arm wrestling each other and doing squats.

Totally lost my thread now. Oh yeah Steve my old mate from school! It's all coming back to me now. So he'd met this poor hotel worker who it turned out was actually a princess but her step mum and two ugly sisters kept her in the kitchens doing the washing up and scrubbing the floors and that but one day a handsome prince came by and … hang on a ruddy minute that's not the story at all that's another fairy-tale! I wonder if anyone has ever done a sweary version of Cinderella. Rhetorical question. Once again unfortunately I run out of time and Internet ink so while I change the ink cartridge you guys think hard about your favourite cheese and the difference between boring and bored but don't any of you dare think about Jet because I've got enough restraining orders out against me to prove my love for that lady. Feel free to bang one out about Hunter or Shadow though. Ooops we didn't get far with the original story today but I have randomly added paragraphs here and there for the moaners even though I love it when some of you more established readers leap to my defence.

I was abandoned by my parents and that makes for insecurity so I admire loyalty. Right then I'm off. I wonder if Jet's little outfit is up on eBay because I have dollars waiting...

I think you've all been very patient - not those tl:tr wankers though they can kiss my lily white arse. Splitters. - Anyway here's the final instalment of, Steve and his multi coloured virginity aka growing up in the country- side part one million. So I've just got back from gallivanting all over the ruddy shop having many adventures and misadventures and taking copious amounts of drugs yet still remaining absolutely gorgeous. My philosophy has always been do anything you like in moderation. I've worked with a lot of people over the years who love a drink and get pissed seven days a week which is fine for a while but not indefinitely because sooner or later you're addicted to the shit and before you know it you're taking cans of cider into work just to stop your hands shaking then it's just a matter of time before your whole life goes down the plug hole. I also know a lot of folks addicted to cocaine. Those miserable paranoid angry mother fuckers. The first time I took cocaine it was offered to me for free while I was at work and at first I said nah you're alright mate but then because I'm me I said, yeah go on then. This was late eighties early nineties and I was a different person back then and I don't think cocaine was even illegal in fact I think it was given away free to poor kids whose parents couldn't afford to feed them so they gave them a gram of Charlie to take away their appetites. That's how I remember it anyway. So yeah I did a line and the next thing I know I'm in my car driving from the West Country up to old London Town. I felt fucking great and as I looked at my Speedo I was doing a ton in my Nissan cherry and my Nissan cheery had never ever done a ton before. I was listening to the red hot chilli peppers and having the time of my life but then I crashed my car and I died leaving thousands of hot chicks howling in despair. I didn't really obviously but I don't want anyone to think that's a cool thing to do. You know coke within twenty minutes it has worn off and as luckily I didn't have any more within no time I was trundling along doing sixty five like a good boy. Back then it was fifty sheets a gram and I could get a quarter of good skunk for that no problem so for me it was just maths. It's a wankers drug anyway and it'll take your soul. But I'm not here to judge anyone each to their own. Women absolutely adore it don't they. That's not a question rule followers. The geezer who gave me my first line was a big time dealer and an absolute minger but his missus was out of this world. You ever see a hot woman with a ugly guy then he's either got a sparking personality or pockets full of bugle. That's a scientific fact. A lot of people got burnt out in the nineties on the old ecstasy and you can still see them around with their dated tattoos and sad craggy old faces. For every up there's a down although not with weed except your short term memory goes but that'll come back. Hopefully mine will anyway. Now where was I? Also not a question. So to sum up all drugs are bad except weed and possibly mdma which is superb ... in moderation. Steve obviously didn't even smoke fags. He drank Cronie and then move on to Pernod and black if he was in for the long haul. He was mental enough already without doing class As and plus as I said there was fuck all drugs to be taken back then. Once me and a mate smoked henna for about a week thinking it was shit hash. I keeled over one tea time and my sister called the doctor because she thought I'd had a fit. Jesus I can still taste it. I also tried smoking potpourri once I don't recommend that either.

So I get back home for a flying visit and meet up with Steve for a catch-up and I say so Steve how's your live life and he says still non-existent but I did go on holiday and I was chatting to this waitress in the hotel and I said good work Steve did you shag her? And he said no because she was religious and couldn't have sex until after she was married and

I said well Steve that sounds not good at all and he agreed and then he said that as she only got about twenty pence a day working in the hotel he was sending her money and rather than say don't do that Steve I said cool because I'm a supportive friend and if I'd said don't do that Steve you mad bastard he would have still done it but he would have been upset with me. It wasn't my money he was sending her and at least he was getting somewhere and plus I loved a good story so I said what's the next step then Steve? And he said that he was going to save up some money and go back to see her. I can feel these too long to read mouth breathers getting all irate now so I'm off ... blame them not me because if it was my choice I'd have finished this story right here and now. I'm off for a quick line and try unsuccessfully to get a hard-on. 😃🍆💧

💧💧

Sometimes I find myself thinking about what Steve's love life would have been like if we'd had the Internet. It's a piece of piss to get laid now compared to the eighties. We had a few pubs and clubs and there was church obviously or the local public toilets but we didn't have the whole wide world at our finger tips. Today you can pretty much type in exactly what type of partner you're looking for into your phone and an algorithm will find you 100s people who exactly fit your ideal and plus they're all local and gagging for it. Without moving from your chair it's perfectly possible to get someone to come to your house have sex with you and then leave. Or stay obviously. Or just stay for a bit. I don't know whatever. Infinite possibilities. We village lads had to organise a designated driver half the time just to try a different pub on the off chance it was full of hot chicks that we'd never seen before. We'd burst in with high expectations and it would obviously just be full of old men and a black lab sat in front of the fire but because we felt obliged to buy a pint and we weren't even that bothered to begin with we'd end up just getting very pissed and going home to fall asleep in front of channel four while having a half-hearted wank. Then we'd talk about it the next night. Especially if we'd all watched the same thing on tv. Which we would have because back then if we hadn't pulled, which we hadn't pretty much always, and fancied knocking one out our wanking materials was very limited. Hang on someone remind me about the Chinese DVD guy. That's in the nineties though. I'm just going to use this one as a note pad. No offence I'm haemorrhaging readers anyway 😊👍 So yeah today I think Steve would have had had no trouble finding a nice young lady to milk his cows with and stroke his mad springy hair that didn't really have any colour to it. I've known Steve since we were about ten and if you asked me what colour his hair was when he was younger I wouldn't be able to tell you. Let's hope that question never comes up. Porno mags, VHS tapes, TV the Sun and the Star and If you were classy the mirror because the page three girls hid their nipples. Actually considering how strict my Nan it was it's surprising that we used to get the daily star every day plus the Sunday people but fair play to her. You could always find something to have a wank about in those Sunday papers. Oops I didn't really push the story forward much in this one did i? Hashtag rhetorical question. I know it must be frustrating but I've just noticed the red triangle in the top left corner of the film I'm now going to watch.

Back in the eighties if you were a teenage boy you had the choice to be a biker, a skin head, a trendy or an indie or if you were Steve, none of the above. Steve got his musical tastes from his parents and liked Genesis and ELO and 10 cc and stuff like that. I'd never really listened to any of it but naturally assumed it was utter shit. I was an indie I was black drain pipes, doctor martins and cardigans. I read the melody maker and listened to the smiths and the pixies and Jesus and the Mary chain and Iggy pop and the Pogues and the Clash and anything that wasn't like that was shit end of. No discussion. Duran - Duran? Shit. Spandau Ballet? Shit. Anything in the charts? Shit. I did like ska though and loved madness and the specials and reggae. I also liked Wham and iron maiden. That was my secret though. Bikers hated the skins and the skins hated the bikers and everyone hated the trendies. Me and another mate were proper musos who thought everything was shit to be honest. I also listened to my mum's old records but unlike Steve's parent's collection hers was ace. Tons of 60's Rock and roll. My mum has been married a lot of times and when the inevitable happened she'd always dig out the country and western sad laments and I loved these too. You should hear me do stand by your man, you'll cry your fucking heart out. There was only one club playing indie stuff and that was miles away but worth the effort. Indie girls. Swoon. Steve never came to these places much though usually because he was playing skittles or darts or snooker or playing the pub's table top computer games which then felt like being in the future but in reality were shit. Steve would say to me, what do you think about her? And I'd say, what Dave's wife? The fifty year old wearing all that makeup and wearing too much perfume? She's horrible Steve and she's got lipstick on her teeth, and I'd picture the two of them at it and laugh in his face and then he'd laugh. I think it must have been because he felt that no girl his age would take him seriously that he found himself looking at the older women or maybe he just liked older women fuck knows to be honest it wasn't my job to get the prick laid and was frankly against my interests. There was only three hot girls in my village and two of them were my sisters so it was every man for himself. We all wanted to be in bands and shag ourselves to death but not Steve. He loved his tractor and his cows more than anything else. Steve was also tone deaf but on occasion he did like to sing out loud which would typically be while we were driving to some old shit hole or another it would always be the same line. Tie your mother down! Tie your mother down! I didn't know who the fuck sang that but I'd always join in. Years later I found out that it was a Queen song; and to this day that's all the lyrics I know. Oh an apropos of fuck all he'd sometimes randomly start singing, I don't like cricket. Oh no. I love it. That was 10cc and I liked that one but he'd only ever utter these few words. He was odd indeed but as he grew older he calmed down a bit and was great company because as I mentioned previously he had no airs or graces you got what you saw. A shout from across the bar, 'Steve, you lost your virginity yet son!?' No not yet Steve would laugh. You ever even kissed a girl? Nope. That was Steve in his early twenties but he didn't give a shit and it never occurred to him to lie or sex up his non-existent sex life and this was refreshing because everyone else was doing exactly that. 'Went in to town last night met some bird banged her all night the next morning she made me breakfast and then I fucked off while she was doing the washing up!' Everyone laughs along even though we all knew it was bullshit. Apart from if I told that story obviously in which case everyone believed it and bought me drinks all night because they knew it was true. 😊I'm old as fuck now but this comes with many positives such as I can now quite openly say what a tune true by Spandau is and the reflex by Duran -Duran and how I felt so sick in my stomach when I heard the news that George Michael had died because I loved him. Actually ELO have a lot of good tunes. Fuck knows about Genesis though apart from that one with the gorilla playing the drums.

Oh yeah Steve and the French supply teacher! ... A moment later a solitary chair was slowly pushed back. Then another then another then another until we were all scuffing our chairs on the floor. That was the final straw.

RIGHT!

She screamed at the top of her lungs angry as fuck.

This actually did the trick and we all sat in our seats shitting ourselves and terrified because we knew she now meant real business. She thought she'd fucking won but she didn't know Steve.

LEFT!

Shouted Steve.

Le Bon Mot.

She couldn't believe it.

This simple but well timed remark was the coup de grace and she didn't have an answer to it. She burst into tears and ran out of the room. We never saw her again and it was never mentioned again. Nobody got punished. We waited for the bell and then we fucked off for lunch. A small victory for us forgotten boys and girls and it was all down to Steve's audacity and disregard for convention. Shit I got side tracked then. Oh well I guess there will have to be a part three then because I've got shit to do. A plus tard.

I wish I could be one of those people that can sit on their own on the beach and just look out to sea contemplating life's absurdities without feeling like a loner slash sex case but I'd be too preoccupied wondering if anyone that saw me thought that I was obviously a loner slash sex case. It's the same with the cinema or going for a walk. I've even thought about wearing a t shirt that says, 'I know what you're thinking but I'm just out for a walk on my own because my wife is at work' but that's a lot of words so the font would be too small for the average passerby to read unless I stood still which would be a bit weird and only add fuel to the flames.

Personally I like spiders around the house around this time of year but if you don't then spray your windows and door entrances etc. with either tea tree or peppermint or vinegar. The latter is the reason you'll never find a spider in a chip shop. That's a scientific fact.

When I see football supporters belting out their national anthems while holding their hand on their hearts I'm really quite envious. I was born in England and I'm English but apart from being an absolute dirge I can never bring myself to sing ours because the words are irrelevant to me. Of course I've got nothing against the Queen in fact I quite like her and back in the day I'd even go so far as to say I would have slipped her a length but as a republican slash stay at home mom slash super model I have never been able to join in with any real gusto. Singing National anthems at sporting events and public gatherings are a fairly recent addition to the world and most were written in the late 18 hundreds. The Italians have a cheer in there's which is well exciting, the USA's is a tune and so is the French one but ours just drags on and on and on and sometimes the game is halfway through before it's over which can lead to a lot of confusion especially when we play Germany and they join in. It's a fucker really because I'm quite a patriotic mother fucker in some ways. If I'm ever coming back from abroad and have a window seat on the plane I always look down and think that England truly is a green and pleasant land and it's absolutely beautiful. I love the humour and the food and the politeness and the sportsmanship and the changing seasons and the music and the birds and loads of other things but the trouble is I've got an awful lot of Celtic blood running through my veins and the English have always been a bit cheeky towards us what with their fixation on expanding their borders and all that malarkey so I've always felt that I've been caught in the middle of an ideological conundrum. I also have trouble fawning over anyone that's not me. I couldn't sing any song about how great someone else is unless it was ironic or I was getting paid to do it. Yesterday I saw the Welsh fans and players all wholeheartedly singing away (in Welsh) and this got them all fired up for the match and when the Scottish team play it'll be the same thing but when it comes to us I'm just going to sit back and let everyone else crack on because nationalism is a cultural concept and I get why it's useful for uniting disparate groups of people and to invoke a bit of passion and patriotism but to be honest it's not really in my preferred key. It's all bollocks anyway and it's always fun to see the players tunelessly mumbling along and also spotting the ones who don't sing at all because they have the same problem as people such as myself. The beautiful irony of all this is that all the way through writing it I've been singing the first few lines of God save the Queen and no doubt that's going to be in my head all day now.

* Cheers in Italian.

Yesterday I spent the day with a bunch - I don't think there's a collective noun yet- of scaffolders. Scaffolders have a bad reputation because usually they are all loud and sexist and sweary and generally deemed to be uncouth, and this lot was no exception. They lived up to every stereotype and more. For a lot of people they can be very intimidating but not for me because I love the anarchy and joy of life they bring to a job. For me they are like pirates. They are unruly and uncompromising and that's because it's an adrenaline fuelled scary job . I asked the loudest one if he liked his job and he said yes of course it's the best job in the world I fucking love it, your job is the worst job in the world and the most depressing. I replied, fuck off you cheeky (banned word) we have the best job in the world fuck doing what you do it's dangerous as fuck and you're all mental. -Don't try this at home folks because there's a fine line and if you gauge it wrong you're going to get thrown off a scaffold by your bollocks/ vagina. -
Then he looked at the guy I was working with who was wearing a t shirt with a camper van on it and said, 'never trust a grown man wearing children's clothes' and it crushed him all to fuck and I laughed my head off because it was beautifully true. My colleague didn't say anything back because this guy

was built like a brick shit house and obviously hard as fuck. In my experience If someone tells you that they are hard or crazy or a lady's man or funny or whatever they usually aren't, the real ones just are and don't feel they need to tell everyone. For example I'm hung all to fuck but I've never felt the need to go around telling everyone because it just exudes. 😏

Builders humour is usually crass and vulgar and cutting and raw but scaffolders take it to the nth degree so never get on the wrong side of one. I'm clearly straight as the come but if I was gay or a straight female, a scaffolder would be my go to, not for marriage obviously but if I wanted a good hard seeing to and then be told to fuck off then it'll be a scaffolder for me all day long. For me A scaffolder's tattoos are much more convincing than all those middle class guys with the beards and little ponytails and fire sticks because you know that they got theirs done while off their nuts and they're all sentimental with their kids names on their necks or the names of their dead relatives and ex-girlfriends and favourite football teams not a sleeve full of whatever happens to be trendy at a particular time and they don't look half as smug either. Don't get me wrong I don't mind tattoos that cost thousands of quids but for me they look a bit too needy. Personally I've been searching for the perfect tattoo for years but I've yet to find it. They say if you want one make a drawing of it and leave it by the side of your bed for six months and if you haven't got bored of looking at it by then get it done. Scaffolders also have millions of kids from millions of different women obviously there are exceptions but I've yet to meet one of the exceptions. These guys pulled up onto the pavement all stinking of weed at 8 o'clock in the morning all laughs and jokes and they continued the day in the same way. Today was boring as fuck in comparison until my mate Daz the Chippie turned up. I hadn't seen him for years. He's also mental and he proceeded to tell that his lungs were fucked and his blood pressure was through the roof and he had a heart condition while rolling a cigarette without a hint of irony. You don't get many old Builders because sooner or later your back is going to go or your knees or shoulders or your neck or you're going to fall off something or die of lung cancer or alcoholism.

It's true I've met a lot of boring and depressed painters. I've worked with more than one that hides cans of beer in his work bag and starts glugging away from 8am onwards and loads that go to the pub every lunch time and snorts a few lines of pub grub and most of the younger ones smoke weed all day but that's the beauty of my Job because even though I don't do any of that one has the opportunity to unlike all of you that work in offices. Most painters are funny as fuck though and we all have the singing voices of angels and for some reason passers-by all seem to think that we are their best friends and when we work in their houses they tell us all their secrets and we laugh all day long and usually actually look forward to going to work. I do anyway

So I woke up, like I do most mornings, and I went down to the kitchen to put the kettle on. I'm a lovely person, one of the best in my opinion because I think I'm naturally nice and so far life hasn't made me all bitter and twisted, plus I even put a bit of effort in just to make sure, but for the first ten minutes or so I need to be left alone because I'm a grumpy mother fucker. I condense all my anger and fury of the futility and casual horror of existence into those ten minutes then I'm happy as Larry for the rest of the day. This is fine during the week because I get up before everyone else so by the time I've got company I've got over myself and I'm all laughs and jokes and positive energy and all that shit. It's more difficult if I'm staying at someone else's house especially if they're already up because it's difficult not to reply to someone's cheery good morning with an expletive and a head butt. What the hell do they mean by, 'good morning?' The sarky wankers. I wish I could just pass them a laminated note that reads, please don't talk to me or acknowledge me in any shape or form until I give you the nod otherwise I'm going to throw you out of the nearest window, please don't take it personally, best wishes and kind regards, Dom. Then hopefully they'd read it, nod to themselves and fuck off.

I've always been a fan of drugs and I've given them all a good go apart from heroin which I'm saving until a doctor tells me that I've got about a month to live then I'll say goodbye to all my loved ones and friends and fly somewhere to where it's good quality and plentiful, get on the brown and then crawl under a bush to die full of opiates. I've thought about this a lot and that's always been my plan. Anyway the second point is, I've already missed the first point but hopefully I'll shoe horn it in later, is that the only drug that I'm truly addicted to is coffee. I'm not even addicted to it because the other day I gave it up for about two weeks without any withdrawals except that life became meaningless. Once back in the day when I was even more beautiful than I am now I was going to the gym five or six times a week and dancing three nights a week I gave up carbs. That was a big mistake. Don't give up carbs. Carbs make you happy. I think it was Kate Moss that said, nothing tastes better than being thin but she was wrong I was thin and toned and on the surface ripped all to fuck but my soul had decided that enough was enough and fucked off. Nothing tastes better than carbs Kate. Fat and happy is my motto these days. Oh yeah point one which was the main point, if you remember I went down stairs to put the kettle on and as I looked into my garden I saw two magpies pulling out strands of fibre from the palm tree and I thought, cool two magpies one for sorrow two for joy happy days. Then I thought do I still have to salute and say, good morning Mr Magpie how's the wife and kids if there's two of the fuckers? Then I thought, why do I still do this when it's evidently just a load of old bollocks? Then I thought of how many occasions someone had been unlucky because they hadn't saluted a magpie when they saw it. A man died today in an explosion because he didn't bother to salute a magpie and ask it about its fucking family. Then I decided that I wasn't going to do it anymore to free myself from the utter madness of it. I feel vulnerable doing this but I think it's for the best. Anyway to cut a long story short if I'm ever round yours and you're up before me keep the fuck out of my way for the first ten minutes unless you're making me a pot of coffee. Don't just give me one cup either it has to be at least a litre and if it's instant don't be surprised if you find yourself getting binned out of the nearest window. If you do that I'll spend the rest of the day making you feel great about yourself and having you in stitches as a way if saying thank you and because for 23 hours and fifty minutes out of every 24 I'm a fucking diamond.

Since re-joining the gym I've seen an awful lot of old men's bollocks and one old man's ass cheeks that will haunt me forever. I really don't know how you birds do it. So much pubic hair too. Jesus I've given myself a soft lob now.

So I come out of the gym, go for a steam then jump in the shower and thank the lord lemon ass guy is not there so there's no awkwardness. Four days on the bounce would have properly messed with his head because I'm sure he already thinks I fancy him because when I'm nervous I don't have a clue what's going to come out of my head until I hear it myself along with everyone else and I've been blurting out innuendos left right and centre during the communal shower and these old posh guys are not my preferred audience they all want to talk about blood pressure pills and Audis whereas I just come across as an amalgamation of all the campest tv personalities from the 1970s who shall remain nameless because I don't know anything about old people's drugs or cars and their banter is proper shit. anyway as if i'm going to be attracted to lemon ass for goodness sake he's twice my age and he's got hairy arms and receding bum cheeks, in his dreams! I'm glad I'm not gay because I couldn't deal with all the hair if I was gay then I'd insist I'm all my sexual partners - and I'd have loads because I'm not one to do things by half - would have to be waxed all over and half my age and ideally Moroccan although I'd consider Italian at a push. Fuck me I got proper distracted then. Anyway so I'm getting changed and while I'm moisturising my feet- this is the only way I can get my socks on- I'm listening to this bunch of squash players banging on and on like something out of that tv program about the old men fucking about in Yorkshire that revolved around a tin bath going down a hill which will remain nameless -but with Received Pronunciation and gout - anyway someone tells a joke, fuck knows what it was but it made me do one of those wry smiles and I looked up towards the direction of from whence it came only to be confronted by a different old man bent over exposing his enormous old bollocks and cock less than three feet away from me... well my instinct was obviously to quickly bang back a gram of Charlie and start beating off like a caged chimp but what I actually did was lock it in my long term memory for some reason. I can't remember what I had for dinner last night but it seems old men's genitalia really seems to stick in my head. Maybe they'd let me post interesting facts on their extremities just to see if I can remember them but I doubt it because they all think I'm an oddball and this would just make it all a lot worse probably. Right then I'm off for a power wank about the whole thing and then try and put it all behind me. Liver spots there's an awful lot of them about too. Keep squatting guys you've got to keep your bum cheeks where they should be for as long as possible or you'll have cheeky little mother fuckers like me writing about you.

* lemon ass obviously isn't twice my age but it's still a no from me. Never say never though that's what I say. I don't really say that. Right then this wank …

I think this one is bereft of celebrities and famous mother fuckers but I wouldn't put money on it because I'm a lazy git.

Good news guys I saw the fellow with the massive bollocks and tiny cock again today. We had a shower at the same time and even though I tried my hardest I'm a very curious man and couldn't help but give him the once over as a lathered myself up. I'd say he was about seventy and the only reason I was checking him out was in order to gauge what I might look like at that age although I was washing my toilet parts rather vigorously at the same time but I suspect that this was just coincidence and nothing to do with my latent homosexuality although I wouldn't be at all surprised if that wasn't exactly the case at all knowing me. Which I do. Anyway the good news is that even though he was about the same age as lemon ass guy his ass was nice and pert which made me feel a lot better about the future of my own buttocks. He still looked old and fucked in many ways but he still had a good set of buns. It was only me and him I'm the changing rooms and I think he remembered me from last time because there was an awkward silence. I'm not good with silence. I'm one of those annoying people who need to fill silence with inane chatter so I thought I'd try and befriend the twat because I'm also extremely insecure due to being abandoned by my mum and that never leaves you. If people don't like me I usually go out of my way to make them like me and then when they do they can fuck off as far as I'm concerned. I'm brilliant at small talk due to being a painter and decorator because we have to do this all the time. Anyway I open with, are you off to the pub now as you've done all the hard work for today and feel you deserve it? A classic after gym quip. He looks at me and I can see him deciding whether I'm worthy of a reply because he's one of those Audi driving middle management twats with a double garage and a holiday home in Portugal or somewhere. Eventually, just before I cave in his head with my flip flops, he chuckles and says, oh no I've got the grandkids coming over. Oh that sounds nice I say, hating myself now for wanting to murder him only seconds before via the medium of cheap rubber. How old are they? Well this batch are one and two. Well they'll keep you on your toes etc. etc. say I apart from the etc. etc. bit which would have been mental so I say, well if you're good to them at least you'll have someone to look after you in your old age, even though he'll probably be long dead before they get to primary school but he perks up at this and says, well that's the idea. And this god awful conversation got me thinking that I should have popped out a shit load of kids when I was younger so the chances of one of the little pricks taking pity on me and building a granny flat on the side of their house for me instead of shoving me in a council run old people's home where I'd get robbed and beaten on a daily basis for constantly shitting and pissing myself would be greater. But I didn't so I'm fucked although my wife is ten years younger than me so I'll be her burden hopefully or due to the amount of drugs I've taken hopefully my brain will turn to mush and I won't know what the fuck is going on until one day I wonder off into the sea in my Jim jams never to be seen again until I'm washed back up in the shore a few miles down the coast and getting poked with a stick by some kid. 'Mum! Come and look at this old dead man's Pert ass cheeks!'

Now I ain't saying that my gym is a hot bed of homo-erotica all I am saying is that I seem to be the only straight guy there. All those young lads in their tight fitting tops and bulging muscles flexing all over the place it's outrageous really and there should be a law against it because I can't concentrate at all. I don't buy into this playing hard to get malarkey either and I know exactly what they're up to but I'm not just a piece of meat or some eye candy for the youth I'll tell you that for nothing. Of course I'll spot you son but first let me help you hold up your weights we don't want that huge thing coming down and bursting all over your face and chest now so we? And another thing I've never understood guys that wear women's black leggings under their shorts (especially if they're German because I don't speak a word of it) If someone wants to cross dress they should do what I do and wait until the missus goes to the bingo, get on the bag, put on her underwear and then lurch and writhe around the bedroom while manically pulling on my ball bag until eventually climaxing all over the cat. If anyone knows how to get stains out of fur then please Dm me before nine thirty at the latest. There's a lot of lads who work out in pairs but unlike when I had friends they never talk to one another because they're all wearing ear buds and listening to music and at times it's like being at one of those trendy silent discos especially as like when I used to go to real discos I always go home alone and have a self-loathsome power wank.

It was a bit boring in the showers today as the only guy in there was someone who I'd chatted to a few weeks ago while in the sauna. Being in a sauna is very much like being in a lift as in it's awkward as fuck but I'm not one for being quiet so I always try to break the ice with some appropriate gags. My favourite one is, fuck me it's like a sauna in here. That's yet to get a laugh but that's probably because it's too intelligentsia for most of the fuckers. Anyway the last time I saw this guy he was saying that saunas are supposed to be good for you if you've had a heart attack and eventually when I'd stopped wondering whether he was flirting with me or just making conversation it occurred to me that he'd obviously had one and this was why he was in the sauna. I'm not good with this sort of thing because I have an over active imagination and I can literally make myself faint just by vividly picturing an event so I made my excuses and fucked off making sure not to make any sudden loud noises on the way out. Thus when I saw him in the shower I didn't immediately jump on his back and make prison jokes for bantz in case he had a stroke. Most of the members of the gym I go to are old as fuck. As I've said before there's a lot of rich old mother fuckers there and it's true what they say about clothes making the man because once those expensive suits are off and they're in their little shorts and t shirts they look just like you and me. Pathetic and obviously in the closet.

I think all the old boys have timed their showers so that they avoid me. The old school romantics. I know that they clearly want to court me like in olden times. Today, what with all these dating apps, fit young lads can hook up within minutes and be at it before you can say mucky Terry is your uncle, but not these old timers, they play the long game and evidently intend to woo me.

I bet they're all thinking that I care that I now shower alone. But I don't. I'm not going to hang around getting all crinkly waiting for one, or ideally three, of them to turn up so they can relive their public school days. Oh no not me so after an hour and a half I quickly get out of the shower and within fifty more minutes I'm all dressed and back in the car not in any way disappointed and really looking forward to seeing my wife who is a woman and I love women what with me being so straight and that.

Today I Will include a bit if grammar and paragraphs for the pedants this time because I'm a people pleaser. 😁 👎

The older I get the more I think about being all fucked up, shitting and pissing myself and going bat shit crazy in the old noggin. This is why I'm always looking at older guys and what shape they're in. Men don't have to push any kids out of their bodies which I've always been grateful for so the only stretch marks I have are around my mouth and they're my own fault from way back in the day when I was a choir boy. I was a beautiful looking kid and when you add the whole choir boy get up you'd have to have been a very devout Catholic priest not to have wanted to commit a few cardinal sins where I was concerned. I was around twenty five at the time and my singing frock was the only one made of white pleather and was covered in studs so in retrospect I only had myself to blame, but I digress.

There's an old guy down the gym who everyone knows and to protect his identity I'm going to change his name to Miguel and now I'm going to change it back to his real name which is Antonio. Antonio is 81 and seems to me to be fit as a fiddle. He's lean and still has muscle definition and he's sharp as a knife mentally and he does spin four times a week. Spin is when you cycle on static bikes under the orders of a gym instructor who motivates you by barking orders at you until you're completely knackered and pleading to just die in order to stop the pain. He's always trying to get me to participate but I've seen them all stagger out of those classes and I've never been one for taking orders plus these days I pretty much hate everyone who isn't me so I politely decline the invitation. Anyway Miguel, not his real name, his real name is Antonio, he's Spanish and has five kids with three different wives and he's got a hefty amount of grandkids one of which is actually a year older than his youngest child. I've never sat down to work this out but I still admire his virility because I am a man and men like to hear this sort of thing because it means that there's a possibility that I won't be some old fart sat in his on piss in front of countdown not knowing what the fuck is going on.

Miguel aka Antonio is the only man I've ever met who says he has a thing for English women. No disrespect to English women I mean that's a broad spectrum and I can't think what a typical English woman would look like. Plus I'm married to an English woman and she's hot as fuck. She's so hot I'm constantly worried that one day she'll look at me and ask me who the fuck I am and why I'm in her house and then start screaming.

Maybe he means their personalities but I don't know what that is or what that would be either. It's more difficult to know these things when you're in the middle of it I think. Typically Most guys will say Brazilian women or Italian or Eastern European or Spanish if they're controlling perverts they'll say Japanese women but I've never heard anyone except Antonio ever mention English women as being their preference. So with this in mind, today when I was in Lidl, I started looking around at all the, what we used to ignorantly call 'female' faces, trying to find the archetypal English rose but as it was Lidl they weren't the best examples and I couldn't be arsed to trudge over to Waitrose.

In other news I now bring my own shower gel which is perfume free kid's shampoo because the stuff they've got in the showers is taken all my skin off.

Cock count today = zero and that includes my own.

I did so quite a few shit tattoos though. One guy, who I think is a porn star, had a tattoo of that dead singer bird on his neck. I think it was her anyway. When's tattoo gets old it's just a blue smudge so fuck knows. There was also some writing but in my experience people don't like you stretching their old skin to see what it says and then correcting spelling mistakes with a marker pen

There must have been a lot of broken hearts at the gym tonight because I didn't go. I did arms yesterday though and then had a quick swim and then I went into the steam room. The steam room is my sanctuary. Well it is if I'm on my own in there otherwise it's a sweaty house of germs. One cough in there and everyone is fucked. I'm not sure if that's actually he case but I can't help feeling it's a bit like the recycled air in planes. One for all and all for one. Apparently on a two hour flight all the passengers have breathed in the same air multiple times so all the burps and farts get sucked up and then regurgitated into everyone's lungs.

This is why you always feel a bit ropey after a flight. You've been breathing in micro doses other people's excretions up to and including kiddy sick, human poo- poo and also all the piss vapours and what have you from the toilets. Nom nom

The last time I went for a swim lemon ass - or someone similar as posh men all look alike when they're naked and wet - was in the pool and he gave me a dirty look because he knew I hadn't booked a lane like some dorky teacher's pet, vegan, nerd, IT consultant, virgin milk monitor electric scooter riding prefect. I'm an anarchist and anarchists do not book lanes they just see that the pool is empty apart from one old man that might've had an office full of minions under him at one time but since he's retired is just another soggy old man with inverted glutes so I just gave him a cheeky wink as I jumped in. He was fucking fuming but not enough to actually say anything to me. I didn't even really want a swim but there's always been a fuck you part of me that I can't control. I only behave like this with arse holes though usually I'm charming and polite but in the presence of controlling bureaucrats I'll go out of my way to upset them.

Hang on I've lost my thread now oh yeah a couple of days ago I was in the changing rooms and these squash twats were banging on and on about fuck all and I'd zoned out but as I was changing from gym me to swim me I was totally naked and in between two of them. Vulnerable but also expectant and excited at the same time isn't a bad state to be in on occasion, anyway one was just your average prick but the younger of the two was quite quiet and much less of a cock and also hench as fuck. I think we all know by now that I'm as straight as they come but i can appreciate a good physique on another man without wanting to start clawing at it in a maniacal Frenzy of homosexual abandonment and besides he certainly didn't miss head day because it was fucking massive.

So he'd just put his gear in a locker and I was thinking great now you can fuck off and take your pal with you when he started to pull on his padlock and that unfortunately was not a euphemism.

He pulled it a few times then walked away then came back and pulled on it again and again and just before I was about to give him the universal look that says,are you taking the fucking piss mate? it suddenly struck me that he was OCD. Like for real.

Many people who claim to be OCD in my opinion are just wankers and rude as fuck and use the term OCD as an excuse for being a wanker and being rude as fuck. But this kid was the genuine article. I counted that he'd clicked that padlock at least 10 times and it suddenly dawned on me what a pain in the arse it must be but on the plus side, because of his OCD, he was fit as fuck.

You see There's people like me that go to the gym because they love the endorphins and being harmlessly naked in front of other men and there's also people like padlock who go because it's soothing for them. I know a couple of guys that are really OCD who go to the gym and have to do exactly the same thing every time and this makes them very muscly so to sum up sometimes when you think someone is being a cock end maybe they're not all maybe they are just coping but mainly if you get into a steam room and I'm already in it I'm going to cough like fuck until you turn around and walk back out ... unless you're lemon ass guy then I'll happily go because I don't want to breath in the hairy moles on your back or inhale your watery old farts. Not unless he buys me a drink first anyway the old rogue.

Sexy gym stories part 8

So lemon ass guy is blatantly playing hard to get as I've only seen him from afar this week and we've not showered together once. This is his loss and I'm sure I could do a lot better anyway. I've been tearing myself apart wondering what it is about me and being ignored by old men and after a lot of soul searching I've had to find to the reluctant conclusion that it's more than possible that neither of us are gay which is a crying shame as I'm sure I'd be very good at it.

Oh well onwards and upwards. In other news I was having my post workout shower a couple of days ago and this young guy is in there, probably between twenty and forty fuck knows to be honest these days I don't have a clue about people's ages. When I was a teenager I could tell if someone was a year older or younger than me no problem but now I could easily go ten or even twenty years either way and still not be sure. I didn't think I ever cared less when up until fairly recently I'd tell someone my age and they'd be all like, no way mate you look much younger than that and then start wanking off or something but now if I'm asked how old I am I tell them and they just nod and it's depressing as fuck to be honest sometimes.

Ain't nothing more ridiculous than a man trying desperately to look younger than he is though that's for sure? You can dress like a teenager but your face will always give you away. It's fun to see though.

There's a bald guy down the gym who must be fifty minimum and he's always working out with younger men and strutting about like a personal trainer barking at them and constantly chewing gum like some teenage fuckwit. You put chewing gum into anyone's mouth and they immediately start acting like a dickhead that's a scientific fact. He reminds me of someone off the tele but for the life of me I can't think who it is which is lucky really because as soon as you mention anyone famous in here regardless of the context the bouncers will whip it out and spank your ass with a copy of the rule book but anyway it ain't complimentary. This prick also dresses like toddler whose parents have just come into a few quid too. Imagine if that ex footballer and his wife who used to be in that girl group had a small child and were made to spend a grand on a gym outfit for it. That's what he looks like. Actually padlock is in his stable of young lads and the two of them were doing chest together yesterday and chewing gum was making all sorts of mad grunts and noises while he was lifting and if that had been anyone else I would have more than likely bashed one out then and there but as it was them I just thought what a couple of plums they were and yearned for my lemon ass crush. Why do they keep glancing over at me I just don't fucking know because I couldn't give a fuck how much they're lifting I just want them to fuck off...

I ain't no fucking head doctor boffin but In my opinion men never ever grow up especially if their mum really loved them and doted on them and for this reason that's why they're always looking for approval. I base this on the fact that in every gym I've ever been in the majority of guys in there are working out and constantly looking around to see if anyone is admiring how hard they are working. Awww mate that's really good you're such a clever boy now then let's get you on the breast, burped and changed and put you down you sad desperate mummy's boy. My mum didn't give a shit about me and I thank her every day for that because when I work out I'm not looking for applause. Every cloud and that eh.

Oh yeah the guy in the shower!

So he was a good looking man I ain't gonna lie, pert ass cheeks, perfect v shaped torso and not an ounce of fat on him and his dick was even bigger than mine but on his head was a bed of wet soapy ginger hair and I know very well that they have their fans but it's a niche market so I came out of there smiling. So to sum up chewing gum should only be sold to teenagers in musicals and those who want to try to hide the fact to traffic officers that they've been drinking. Right them I'm off to Gap kids to get suited and booted. 😎

Guess how old I am?

Couldn't give a fuck mate.

* Actually if anyone asks you this always go at least ten years higher than you think that way they will fuck off a lot quicker.

Heeey Fonzie!

I think padlock and chewing gum have fallen out due to chewing gum training another boy who I shall call bones due to him being very skinny. Bones also plays squash and has at least three rackets which I'm my opinion is excessive. Bones also wears a hair band like that footballer man who also wears one. Men wearing hair bands are an increasingly common sight these days. Hair bands and not wearing socks.

I think there's some kind of squash inner circle because they all come into the changing rooms all full of themselves charged up on endorphins and shit golf stories.

As far as I can tell faded prison tatts sees himself as the governor due to his shit tattoos and cockney accent. I've never heard so many stories without any punch lines and nobody knows when to laugh which is awkward.

I'm a decorator and if I go to the gym straight after work I'll be wearing decorator clothes which I'm my case is a pair of white decorator's trousers and a white t shirt. Classic painter wear. The other day I was getting changed and chatting to this bathroom tiler at length about this and that for about twenty minutes until I was fully clothed and he suddenly asked me what I did for a living. I thought he was taking the piss so I laughed because it was quite funny but it soon became clear that he wasn't joking. Next time I will take in some brushes and some paint just so it's more clear.

Some middle class people react very oddly in this gym when they see a member of the working class. Usually they just throw me a disdainful glance or become condescending but my favourite is when they suddenly turn into that public school educated English film director who married that American pop star and start giving it the old gawd blimey love a duck act as if I give a shit where they come from. This one guy was talking to his mate and then glanced at me and suddenly became the chimney sweep character out of that film with the actress who played a posh people's nanny and started loudly telling a story about how he was in a club and thought that the bouncer called him an effing c and was just about to knock him sparko and his mate thought the bouncer called HIM an effing c and was also going to knock him the f out but it turns out that that wasn't the case at all. Like I said no punch line and his mate didn't know if he'd finished the story and there was this dreadful silence which was the only highlight of his shit story. If he'd told that story on a building site he would have been ripped to pieces and thrown in the slip. He was also wearing a hair band come to think about it and he reminded me of a very butch school girl.

Chewing gum asked bones if he was staying on to do legs with him but bones said he was meeting someone and they were going to play Nintendo round his and chewing gum looked sad and lonely for a brief moment. Then he took his ear bud case and sulked off to the changing rooms. Bones pissed about half heatedly working out until enough time had passed until it was assumed chewing gum had left the building then fucked off himself.

I was left looking at myself in the big wall mirror as I was on the cables. Either side of me was a teenage kid Hench as fuck or at that moment I'd never felt so old. Apart from the last time this happened.

I always tell anyone who needs to hear it that comparison is the thief of happiness so I took my own advice for once and immediately cheered myself back up.

I'm sure that one of the personal trainers think I fancy him but the truth is I'm always wondering how many of his clients he's shagging. The older women flirt like fuck with him right in front of their husbands who try not to get the arse or cringe in embarrassment. There aren't any female personal trainers but I know that men behave in exactly the same way. I never judge. I just observe and try to be objective because between sets there's fuck all else do do except people watch ... Comparison is the thief of happiness ... comparison is the thief of happiness... I think lemon ass guy should see the doctor about all the moles on his hairy back because I'm sure some of them are getting bigger. He should also squat but folks don't like to be told these things so I keep my gob shut and fuck off home

So yeah I now like padlock. He was all wet and smiled at me while pointing to his locker which was right next to mine. Everyone's locker is always next to mine. Every single time. No matter where I go in that changing room whichever one I choose there's always at least ten people either side of it. I don't even remark upon this fact anymore because it's so common I just slide all my stuff to one side as whoever it is drips all over the place. It's less sexy than it sounds.

The only thing less sexy than a naked pensioner is a wet naked pensioner. Before I went to this gym I went to another one which was a chain and I think has now folded but the quality of human man was a lot higher although admittedly they were even more twattish.

Young fit men in my experience are often thick as shit. The more handsome the less of a personality. I think it's nature's way of being fair. Beautiful people don't need a personality because they are beautiful and that's usually enough to get them by until they've reproduced and it's only as they get older that they find themselves plain and dull and then they're fucked but it doesn't matter because they've carried on their beautiful genes.

Less beautiful people need to try a lot harder but this stands them in good stead as they age. I mean I ain't no biological scientist but I do have a city and guilds in painter and decorating so mama didn't raise no fool. Well mama didn't raise me at all but this is neither the time nor the place for that.

So yeah I came bouncing into the changing room just as padlock came back from his mad shower. I didn't know what the fuck was going on because only his top half was wet. I immediately thought that only having half a shower was part of his ocd ness and didn't really question it any further. what I will say though is that he, unlike the majority of those dad's army looking end of life corpses looked hot as fuck wet.

Now I'm a straight man I think that's been made very clear but young padlock has a beautiful v shaped torso and big muscles all over, couple that with his wet eye lashes then even I was weighing up the pros and cons of living with someone who has to carry out pointless tasks all the time just to stay sane. I decided no if only because my wife wouldn't like it at all and she's a lot harder than me and could easily fuck me up if provoked plus there was a good chance that padlock wouldn't stay like that forever and one day he'd look like lemon ass and all covered in hairy moles and liver spots so I kept my powder dry and did not invite him out to the famous Portuguese chicken restaurant for a two for one followed by no holds barred frenzied bare back love making.

Now I know that a lot of human women find a man in grey joggers that show off his pulsating meat ticket a love plums a massive turn on and padlock was sporting a pair of these and furthermore they were wet due to his half shower and as I watched him bouncing all over the changing rooms full of post work out vim and vigour I thought to myself, ' sooner or later I'm going to have to change my sweat towel and wash my workout gloves because even though I'm like a dog who loves the smell of his blanket sometimes enough is indeed enough' this thought was also provoked by the fact that the other day I gave some kid in the gym spuds while wearing these bacterial ridden things and after five to ten days all his STD's cleared up.

So yeah it's been a while, fuck knows why everyone starts a sentence with so these days but fuck it, it is what it is one must try to keep up with the trends.

I ain't gonna lie and to be fair are also very popular around my way but let's crack on and not fly off on too many tangents this early in the game because I know that many of you mother fuckers see something that's not a meme or more than three words and think to yourselves, fuck that I don't have time to read all that shit I need stuff to be short and sweet because I've got shit to do and then before you know it's eight hours later and you're balls deep inside a friend of a friends holiday photos cracking one out while off your nut on ketamine and monster trying not to accidentally press the love icon on a photo of someone's Nan in Spain taken back in the seventies when she was hot or replying to a comment that's got fuck all to do with you and is five years old.

Fuck me one needs to be very careful what one writes these days because everyone seems to have a highlighter in their hands waiting to spot something that's offensive to them, 'you sick fuck my next door neighbour's cousin was addicted to ketamine and cheap red bull you heartless, unthinking mother fucker!' It's just words and comedy and when it's comedy then it's comedy and not real life although I'm a rude mother fucker so I would naturally say that to justify my rudeness now wouldn't I.

I miss those pre- Internet days sometimes because the only people that you spoke to were your friends and if they found something offensive you'd just tell them to fuck off and stop being such a needy little cry baby and then kick the shit out of the little nerds and have their dinner money away and that would be that. it was ace. A lot less porn though and you had less opportunity to have a wank over your best friend's life partner so it's a game of two halves really.

Oh yeah the gym! Well I've seen a lot of old male genitals recently. I mean a fuck of a lot. Big ones, small ones and some as big as your ruddy head if you've got a head like a big old saggy ball sack covered in liver spots.

Back in the day I used to go to a sexy gym pretty much everyone was sexy as fuck because we were all of an age where we were all looking to get laid. Everyone was taught and tight and buff and clean and there was no grey hairs about and the tattoos looked new. Well there was one old guy that used to help out all the young girls and try and persuade them to go to the steam room with him but we all knew he was a dirty old bastard and his oily charms only ever worked on me.

I remember being on a job once and one of the chippies was telling us all about this club he went to at the weekend and he was about twenty five and I was eighteen or something and me and my mate were all like, what the fuck is that old man going to a club for? The perv. 25 is not old and neither is thirty or forty even. I actually look at forty year olds now and think, wow look at you you've got your whole life ahead of you.

This fucking gym I'm at now just reminds me of the fact that sooner or later we are all going to die. Horribly and in a lot of drawn out pain probably.

I'd like to think when I retire I won't be trying to stave off the inevitable by staggering about on a treadmill or playing racket ball with a bunch of other absolute deluded wankers no way not me I'll be one of those don't give a fuck, thong wearing, sex tourists hanging out the back of and snorting cocaine off hot teen lady boys … as long as I can square it with the wife obviously.

Oh yeah that reminds me off a chat I was having with a guy in the changing rooms only yesterday. It turned out that We both enjoyed dancing and I said if you see a hot woman with an ugly old man he's either got a few quid or he can dance. *In the comfort of the confines of a changing room one can say horrible old clichés like that without needing an admin to break up a verbal punch up. It turns out that this old rascal had three girlfriends on the go at the same time and I thought to myself, you're obviously not married to someone like my wife who would not even tolerate one, even a small one like a circus dwarf but as he was even older than me I contented myself with the thought that they must be proper minging. 'Oh my God please do not assume these ladies are minging all women are beautiful! Admin!'

Okay fat then.

… Fuck it never got around to telling you all about the latest on chewing gum and padlock. Oh and there's an update on wing bitch too but that's for another time I guess. I'm off too look for discarded

149

porn mags that have been thrown from cars. I wonder if jazz mags will ever come back into fashion like cassette tapes have. To be fair I'd be very surprised if anyone finished all this shit, I ain't gonna lie.

My favourite thing to do in the gym is finish working out have a shower then sit in the steam room and sweat. It's like church for me. I sit in there and contemplate my life and think of all the stories I will one day write. This contemplation is usually interrupted by other people having the audacity to join me but I'm a very sociable young man and as I'm a writer I can't help interrogating people just in case they've got something interesting to say. For a man, unless it's anything the kids or my wife or the guy I work with is saying, I'm also a very good listener so I've picked up quite a few good little snippets over the years. Unfortunately I can't remember any of them but if you were talking to me you'd never guess that even though I was listening intently I wasn't taking anything in at all. I've heard loads of good stories over the years but unless some kind of stage hypnosis person can get them out of me they're gone forever. So that's that fucked.

The other day I walked in and there was this big ginger mountain of a man in there covered in tattoos so I immediately got my dick out and started beating off like a caged chimp. Not really I just said hello and started chatting away. It transpired that he was a policeman. I was prepared this time because the last time I asked someone what they did for a living and they said they were a policeman I instinctively took a step back and looked fucking horrified while unconsciously patting myself for drugs which the guy took to be some kind of admission of guilt although we did become sort of pals until I drunkenly whipped his ass playing ping pong in a Turkish holiday resort and he got the right hump and that was that. This time however I said something like, cool that must be a lot of fun especially if you're a physchopath or a racist! He looked at my dead in the eye and I ain't gonna lie there was a bit of tension in the air but luckily for me it was sexual tension and after a while we both giggled like two shy geisha girls and whipped out our dicks and started beating off like two cages chimps although to be honest due to his colouring he looked more like an orangutan with challenging behaviour.

Anyway it turned out that he was alright and told me a few good stories that I can no longer remember.

Another time a gypsy and his son came in and immediately started covering themselves in baby oil. well I've watched enough gay porn to know how this was going to end so I immediately whipped out my ... hang on that's the intro to the homoerotic wank I'm going to have later, please forgive me.

I know two things about gypsies one is that their sons are always Chubby and two, they all support Manchester United. That's a scientific fact and if you don't believe me go google it. Oh and I've never met a gypsy that wasn't extremely polite. So the dad offered me some baby oil and if I knew anything it was that if a gypsy offers you baby oil in a steam room you jolly well except it. So I said, ooh yes please, like it was the most natural thing in the world to be in a steam room oiling myself up with a father and son gypsy combo. It wasn't as sexy as it sounds but it was still a bit sexy. Two days later here they were again and the same thing happened and so I found myself once again covered in baby oil talking football and boxing. Apparently a gypsy will never rob a car that has a pair of boxing gloves hanging from the rear view mirror. Also a fact. I enjoyed their company but I don't want to see them again because that oil was playing havoc with my t zone and I know that I'm too much of a wet lettuce to tell them no thanks because the whole scenario is completely messed up.

Another time I walk in and there's these two teenage lads in there which also sounds like the wanks I've been having lately but this was a real situation and I was listening to them banging on about their skin regimes, one had greasy skin and spots and the other apparently had combination skin and I was thinking that back when I was their age if I mentioned to any of my mates about the state of my skin I would have been murdered to death with a combined harvester. In fact I mentioned this to them and said how refreshing it was to hear lads talk of such things these days. it was a compliment but they clearly took this as flirtation and immediately whipped out their dicks and started beating off like two polite, albeit rather intimidating, oiled up spotty gypsies.

... Anyway I came out and all my tin had vanished.

Fuck it I forgot about padlock et al again. Oh well next time I'll finish this off for good. I'm off for that wank if I can find any baby oil.

Sexy gym diaries; A Mother's Day special.

So good news! I saw another guy today in the changing rooms with exactly the same mad looking inverted bum cheeks as lemon ass. He was about the same age and wearing very colourful dung hampers. Just as I resigned myself to thinking that this was an inevitable result of age regardless of how many squats a fella could do to ward this off he turned around and low and behold it was actually lemon ass. It was all I could do to stop myself from going over to him and giving him a hug and saying, lemon ass! Thank fuck it's you blud clart! There's still hope! Then I remembered that he doesn't know I call him lemon ass so I didn't; plus that's not good gym etiquette especially as he was still a bit damp. Hugging damp people has never been my thing. The other day I was introduced to the foreman on a building site and as we shook hands his was limp and wet and I knew then that we could never be real friends. He was quite the character though and immediately went into a thousand different tangents while I just stood there wishing I had a pen or a decent memory because it was both disturbing and fascinating at the same time. 'Fuck me we're quickly disappearing into some kind of rabbit hole here.' I say.

I quickly get that he's one of these conspiracy theorists and a flat earth mother fucker and everything I thought I knew was actually the opposite.

There's so many nutters on building sites that this was all just par for the course and all I wanted him to do was fuck off and stop

clearing his throat and spitting all over the room I was working in.
'You're a fucking loony tunes aren't you mate?' I say.

Not in a horrible way. it's hard to describe how we talk to each
other on building sites it's all very un pc and there's no diplomacy or
politeness after the first initial greetings. Once it's established that
you're not a prick everyone relaxes and we all take the piss out of
each other to within an inch of our lives. This can be very
disconcerting to the uninitiated.

I over hear two Chippies asking the new labourer if he's a
homosexual and if so would he like to bum them. The offer is
politely declined. Last week when I wasn't there apparently one
Labourer turned out to be a gay porn star that was making bundles
doing that only fans thing and when another labourer found out that
he was gay he got the hump and fucked off. This was very unusual
because usually builders are very open minded folks.

I'm a writer and so when I see someone with a bit of a personality
I'll interview them in case I learn something new and the new
labourer was an excellent interviewee. Turns out that he was a drug
dealer up in London but his mate got jelly about his success and his
fit cock head bird so told a bigger drug dealer where he kept all his
drugs so they went Round with guns and took the lot and he had to
then fuck off for his own safety.

There's a lot of bull- shitters on site but I believed him. He told me
all about the new drugs that the kiddies are on these days and what
his mark-up was. After overheads he'd be clearing 5 k a week tax

free. Now he was a labourer earning considerably less. Still alive though.

It turned out that the foreman was bi-polar. You taking medication for that mate? I say. Knowing the answer really. 'No fuck that I ain't gona to be no fucking zombie!' He replies then coughs up some horrible shit and spits it on to the floor. I give him a look like, are you fucking mental mate!? And out of respect for me he stamps it with a boot as if that's the most polite thing to do. I like him though because he's harmless enough and he'll be a character in one of my novels so it's all good. He tells me so many things in such a random way that I eventually switch off and eventually he fucks off.

For the rest of the day we play this game of switching the radio station from 6 music to Smooth. I like six music but the DJ's get on my tits; old men trying to be cool. 'Oh my God dad stop embarrassing me! What do you mean I bet all your friends wish their dads were as cool as me! No they do fucking not fella. No they do not. I like to sing all day so Smooth is my go to and he can fuck right off.

Chewing gum and prison tatts come into the gym trying to give it the large one then hand stand starts standing on his hands and when the two plumbers or whatever they are come in I decide to take my leave.

Two gypsy boys are in the steam room and look very furtive as I enter. Mercifully they leave after a minute and I can now lay down and contemplate life. Five minutes later I hear one of them in the pool. He clears his throat and spits into the water. I decide that all decency has gone from the world, shit on the floor, eat it and leave with my dignity intact.

Happy Mother's Day one and all.

I saw a discarded tampon in the road today. It's been ages since I'd seen one and I felt quite nostalgic. Hoping for a rubber Johnny tied in a knot next.

For some reason, I've never understood, Carpet fitters always think they're the bollocks.

I remember when I used to think kids were cute. I'd be all like, hey baby look at that little kid being cute! Now, unless they are a blood relative, they properly get on my tits. This morning we were in MacDonald's and i wasn't even in a bad mood because I'd just beaten my wife at pool which is increasingly rare these days anyway I ain't a massive fan of takeaway food but on occasion those breakfast MacMuffin mother fuckers are the proper dollars so this dad comes in with a brat on one of those little push along bikes and I'm not a Tory but I'm thinking get off the bike dick head this ain't your back garden anyway he's fucking about and making this odd squeaking kind of sound and looking my way and grinning manically all wide eyes and off key and bouncing his bike wheels all over the gaff and his dad is just ignoring him and just when I was going to point him out to my wife and remark on what a little prick he was he fell off his bike and landed on his face and I laughed out loud. I've said it many times ... always remember that however brilliant you think your kid is everyone else who's not their Nan thinks they're a horrible little wanker. No exceptions. Yeah, yeah but my little lad is a rascal but ... nope. He's a prick too. No exceptions

I think it's hard not to become a bit of a twat when you get past a certain age because your opinions, however mental and deranged, become solidified if you're not careful. It's better to always at least try to be flexible and willing to change your mind i feel; but it's difficult when everyone else your age becomes a bit smug and full of themselves because they've got a double garage and a loft conversion and a time share in Spain or whatever and this seems to give you the right to become a dick and have dickish opinions about things you don't really understand. These days I'm chatting to people and thinking, you're a fucking idiot mate how the fuck do you own a detached house? Why aren't you living in a box under a bridge? Not even your own box. A borrowed box you begged off your ex-wife who felt sorry for you?

One day you're cool and free because you don't know fuck all about anything and just happily wing it then you become mature and form opinions and the next thing you know you're chatting absolute shit but with conviction. No wonder young people think old people are wankers.

Young people also get on my tits but at least they've got good hair and tight skin and as they're banging on about whatever they're banging on about and boring the shit out of you, you can marvel at how well they look compared to you and remember when you also looked beautiful but didn't know it at the time. I think Proper old people are usually cool though because they've given up giving a fuck and are just chilling until death takes them.

So to sum up, it's Middle aged people that need to give their head a wobble and young people look good but they are dull. I could be wrong though but as I'm middle aged I couldn't care less about other People's opinions unless they are exactly the same as mine.

Sexy gym diaries. The good, the mad and the anxious.

I'm back down the gym and loving it again. I had some mad migraine and anxiety attacks type of craziness but I'm fine now. I had to have an MRI which put the shits up me but it's all done and dusted now. One's mind is a dangerous thing when it's suddenly working against you. Mine was anyway. I could be in a shop or at work minding my own business when I'd suddenly feel like I had to get the fuck out or I'd faint or die or both. Totally irrational feelings I've never experienced before. It all started when I went to see a ear nose and throat consultant because I developed tinnitus and loss of hearing in my right ear. I was fine when I walked in but totally fucked by the time I walked out. I was all like, doc babe it's probably my sinuses or an allergy or hay fever so let's all just forget it but he was all like, no way man it's not any of that we need to get you an MRI and see what the fuck is really going on my dear! He kept calling me my dear which was a bit sexy at first but when I realised it was a cultural thing I reluctantly put my dick back in my pants. Do you get headaches and dizziness my dear? Nope. Says I. Do bright lights and loud music give you blinding headaches that make you just want to lie down in a dark room while your heart beats out of your chest baby doll? No sir it's just a ringing in my ears and I'm a bit mutton in my right ear. He looked disappointed. Don't worry sugar tits 70 % of people with your symptoms do not have a massive brain tumour the size of a cricket ball pulsating inside your brain which could kill you at any given moment... sweet lips... He continued. I think that's what he said but I was now sweating like fuck and trying not to faint. I walked out of that appointment in a daze. The next day I started to get a migraine which seemed to last for about a month I then started feeling dizzy and getting panic attacks. I've always been chilled as a mother fucker so this came as a surprise to me. My over active imagination is usually a good thing because I'm a writer but when it turns in on itself it's my worst enemy. Anyway I was pretty much living on a knife edge until I had the MRI and eventually got the all clear. The experience has made me value my life more than anything else that's happened to me before including dying for a couple of minutes one new year's Eve and it's also made me a lot more empathetic towards people who have panic attacks and mental health issues. Fuck that it's horrible and it's uncontrollable and frightening. The good news for me is that it went as soon as I got the all clear and I'm back to my happy go lucky self again but I don't take my health for granted anymore and I value life. That sounds a bit wanky but it's true. I took the time to watch a squirrel scampering about today and I saw Dave the pigeon; I saved its life once and it still won't fuck off. It was lumbering about trying to land on a branch without looking like a right dick head and I worried he'd never settle down and find a bird of his own as he's still hanging about with his mum and dad. Three's a crowd Dave I told him. He's thick as shit but I still love him and worry about him. So yeah I walk into the gym and I see the little guy who stands on his hands and walks about waiting for the applause that he will never get, the big fucker who uses all of the gym equipment at the same time and never wipes any of it down like he owns the gaff and my new crush who is ninety but only looks about seventy. He's got more hair on his bonce than I had even when I had hair. I then go to the sauna and listen as two working class lads discuss going over to Russia and topping Putin which I found both sweet and sexually arousing. I then shower and fuck off and who do I see at the top of the stairs but chewing gum. He reluctantly waits for me to climb up and I reluctantly say thanks. It's the first time I've ever spoken to the prick. We both nod but we both think the other one is a wanker and I smile to myself because I know order has been restored and I've missed him because he symbolises routine and normality and that's what I've missed. Oh yeah my favourite part of the day was moments after I left the showers this old boy walks in and as I'm drying my toes he lets out the most enormously loud wet fart and shouts, yes!

Which had me giggling all the way to Lidl's where I bought a potato ricer. The sun shone and as I drove past all the daffodils and crocuses on my way home I felt good. Normal is good.

Sexy gym diary. Winter Olympics special.

I only manage to get down the gym once a week lately due to not giving a fuck about going to the gym. I'm no boffin but I think that humans are programmed to stay in during the winter months and eat shit loads of carbs and sugary snacks to stop you from topping yourself until spring. The other day I was drudging into work and saw some crocus ... croci? Crocuses? Nobody knows ... anyway they cheered me right up because I knew that sooner or later this eternal winter would end eventually. Last Saturday I went to the gym and then to the steam room. I love the steam room. The steam room is where I do all my best thinking unless someone else is in there. I hate other people being in there. Why can't they go in there some other time? Selfish fuckers. I have had a few conversations in there though but you have to keep going out to cool down and it breaks up the flow then nobody can remember what the fuck we were talking about anyway that session was ruined even further by the bird teaching babies to swim outside in the pool she sings to the little twats and those songs get deep into my very core and the next thing I know I'm in Lidl singing about waving my hands and shaking my bottom to all and sundry. I've fucked it off this week to watch the curling final.

I'll be glad to see the back of the curling. The only trouble with curling is that it's shit. Skittles, now that's a good game, especially after a few pints. Drunken skittles on ice is the future. Bloody curling. If you don't sweat it's not a sport. You'd sweat if you played drunken ice skittles though especially if you snorted a few lines of bugle and had a tear up with your opponents in the car park afterwards. I'm off to get lottery money funding for drunken ice skittles. Actually skittles is also pretty shit now I've thought about it. What they should do is combine all the Winter Olympic sports into one event and get it out of the way in the first morning so that there's more time to watch repeats of the chase and them hairy biker lads. Is it me or do people from Newcastle speak like over enthusiastic three year olds? I know they're all hard and that but you ain't ever going to get one on university challenge. Actually I don't think I've ever heard a regional accent on university challenge. We never did 18th century painters or Latin or hard maths questions or philosophy or sub atomic atoms and all that malarkey at my school all we did was copy shit from the blackboard and try not to get our heads kicked in so fuck knows why I watch it. My only chance is if they do a pop music question from the eighties and even then the answer is always Bjork. I miss when athletes were all full of Russian drugs I think that's where I get my kink for women with facial hair and a pair of bollocks from. If there was more hot birds in leotards snowboarding while shooting pandas then I'm sure their ratings would go up. Curling? Fuck off.

Wave your arms, shake your bum that's the way to have some fun... it's not though not in Lidl it's the way to end up getting your head kicked in. Probably get away with it in Waitrose though but fuck knows because it's been years since I've been in one and even then it was just to have a break from people like me for a bit.

Spiritualists and mentalists used to pretend to eat glass on stage but it was really ice cubes. They'd also often say that members of their audience had a scar on their right knee because apparently most people do. I don't though. Oh yeah and the mediums would send flowers to their congregation and the delivery guy would nip in to the house nick something then next time they saw them they would produce the item on stage and say that late auntie Jean or whoever found it. The bounders.

I've never travelled first class on a train but I do get why first class travellers get the arse if you're clearly sat in there without a first class ticket. If I could afford to sit somewhere away from people like me then I most definitely would.

Shit you didn't know that you wanted to know until now

2 why does 'kettle' mean watch in Cockney rhyming slang.

Ahem, perhaps the most confusing of all rhyming slang expression, because the derivation of Kettle from the word "watch" is unclear - until you know a little bit about the history of watches that is. Kettle is the shortened form of Kettle and Hob. When pocket watches first became fashionable, they were held against the body by use of a small chain. The watch then slipped into the pocket and could be easily extracted without dropping it. These were called fob watches, and it's from this expression that we get Kettle and Hob for watch. Kettle and Hob. Fob... watch

Calm down it won't always be Cockney rhyming slang. In fact it could be any random old shit depending on that's going on in my mind at the time.

According to boffins, the best car to have sex with is a Toyota Yaris.

Shit you've always wanted to know but didn't know that you wanted to know it until now.

#1 why is 500 quid called a monkey by cockneys and gangsters off the tele?

The term was coined by British soldiers returning from India where the 500 rupee note of that era had a picture of a monkey on it. They used the term monkey for 500 rupees and on returning to England the saying was converted to sterling to mean £500. And as a bonus ... The twenty five rupee note had a pony on it. Tune in next time for more, shit you've always wanted to know but didn't know that you wanted to know it until just then. Or whatever it was.

Four out of ten Americans believe in psychics. One out of ten British people believe in psychics.

Mime artists, figure skaters and vegans will all ruin any drug you've just taken.

Sometimes when I'm out and about I see people smiling to themselves and if it's a woman I often think, aww what a lovely thing to do and if it's a man I often think, sex case.

You definitely need ear pods on a train full of students. Sheesh.
How grown up people can teach these fuckers without killing
them all is beyond me. I know that they are all just scared
humans trying to fit in and choice of genders these days is now
so over whelming and all that. I do get it. I struggled with the big
four way back in the eighties and I'm still not a hundred percent.
 if only there was one where they shut the fuck up for a bit or at
least got me to write their lines so it wouldn't be so dull. I had a
film studies tutor at university once who was always trying to
shag his students but personally for me it would have been too
high a price to pay. Yeah you've got tight skin and soft pubic
hair but fuck me I don't want to hear any of your opinions about
anything. Ever. Please leave and don't forget your bag with all
those crap badges on them. Then I'd just have a wank about
them and date someone only a mere ten years younger than me
because old people get on my tits too.

Edinburgh nights.

An opinion based on empirical evidence and boffin data.

Remember in the olden times when you could go to places that weren't just up the road or your mum's ? Well me and the missus did just that at the weekend. We recycled some cardboard and tins to offset our carbon footprint and flew up to Edinburgh. It was fucking cold, like proper cold but I fell in love with the gaff. Now I'm an ex-Catholic and shouldn't morally have enjoyed it but I did. I'm half Scottish and my lot are from Glasgow. it's only a few miles inland but it's totally different. Less violent and by that I mean both physically and in tone. The Glasgow accent is much more threatening and if someone asks you the time your instinct is to immediately hand over your wallet and your bird's engagement ring but the Edinburgh accent is much softer although still rather abrupt compared to my southern bastard one. There's no passive aggression to the Scots they call a spade a spade and for me that's refreshing you know where you stand and that's the way I like to do business. Masks are still mandatory and if you enter a shop without one they immediately ask if you've got one and when you say, yes I think I've got one somewhere they say, well put the mother fucker on then dipshit or get the fuck out. This didn't happen to me because I always wore one because I'm not an entitled dick head plus it helped kept the fucking cold out a bit. They sure did burn a lot of witches back in the day and they loved a bit of torture too. Single woman? Witch. Left handed? Witch. Curly hair? Witch. Don't eat your crusts? Witch. Unlike Glasgow they don't overtly hate the English in Edinburgh this is because ninety percent of its occupants are posh English students and the other ninety percent are Chinese. Chinese loud Japanese polite that's how you can tell them apart. That's scientific boffins not me and boffins don't lie that's why they're boffins. Edinburgh is where that dog Bobby slept by his owner's grave until he died and they gave him his own grave and people leave toys and sticks and other general dog related stuff by the side of it which is totally normal. I learnt that the phrase, to get shit faced, originated in Edinburgh and it goes like this, back in the day, before toilets were invented, people used to throw their waste out of their windows into the street below at ten pm with a cry of garde l'eau! Which is French is for, ,watch out muggy!' Or some old bollocks but let's say you were coming back from the boozer and you heard a cry from above you might instinctively look up and get yourself a face full of shit you see? I loved that. Grave robbing was all the rage too and Burke out of notorious body snatchers and serial killers Burke and Hare can be found in the medical museum behind a glass panel. Well some of his skin anyway because he was flayed and made into a lovely note book. I ate my first oyster which was ok to be fair, a bit like swallowing lumpy spunk but without feeling obligated to have a cuddle after. Lots of ghost stories and Protestant history and bag pipes in the street and photos of the queen and prince Phillip dotted about. Their Cathedral looks a bit sparse compared to Rome but I guess that's the whole point anyway I lit a candle for me Nan and dropped fifty pence in the collection box rather than the suggested fiver, tenner or twenty quid. Cheeky bastards. There's only one person who can put you in your place better than the Scottish when you're trying to give it the large one about wearing a face mask and that's a homosexual flight attendant. Bloody English proper get on your tits sometimes don't they? I know I certainly do.

I'm back down south now and it's positively balmy down here. No haggis were harmed in the making of this load or old random bollocks. I could live up there but only during the summer months or when the English have all fucked off back to their mummy's and daddy's estates. Yesterday me and the wife where in some Vietnamese street food type joint and the two posh English birds sat on the next table where so loud and pleased with themselves about fucking fuck knows that we had to move to the opposite side of the cafe. I know it's because I'm jealous that they still think life isn't utter shit and know nothing of existentialism but even so they were putting me off my fucking noodles. Oh yeah iron bru goes with everything. Everything.

I've needed a piss for about an hour now but I really can't be arsed with it all. Lucky for me I've never given birth out of one of those vagina things birds have so I can also laugh my head off without fear of getting wet legs. I still wear a Tena lady though but only for sexy reasons I won't go into right now. As you were.

You can tell if somebody is a serial killer (especially the cannibal ones) by their haircut and the colour of the lenses in their glasses. That's science and boffins don't lie, that's why they're called boffins. FYI a thick black fringe and yellow lenses ... run for your lives.

Eating soup without bread is a sin obviously and when I was a kid I'd have butter on my bread but then without me knowing it I became middle class and started calling tea dinner and dinner lunch and not tucking my shirt in and this and that … I never got my head around supper because that's just madness as unless you're a psychopath nobody eats that late unless they enjoy indigestion… unless cheese is involved obviously. Oh yeah I also stopped having butter with my bread but now as I've clearly become class conscious again I'm back on the butter. Not those nut job alternatives either just proper full fat salted butter. If I'm going to have a heart attack due to dairy products I'm going down laughing. Butter is love. Spread the love. I'm glad I wasn't born in the age of the vegan. I don't have an opinion on them and I actually think it makes a lot of sense but it's not for me. Not right now anyway. Today you've got your vegan which must be shit but on the plus side you've got your pan sexuality to make up for it. 'Yeah I know I can't wear a leather jacket or doctor martins or eat honey but when I go down the pub I can try to fuck anything I like without getting my head kicked in' … the lord give us and the lord takes away … and I think the hours are better too…the lucky bastards…

Sexy gym diary. Part 99

January is a shit month of the year that's a scientific fact. If you
ask the boffins what the shittiest month of the year is they will do
some calculations in a big computer and that computer will make
loads of clanking sounds and eventually a piece of paper will
then come out of it and on that piece of paper will say, January.
Today is officially the shittiest day of the year. That's boffins not
me so I will have no dissent in the ranks. The good news is that
it's all downhill from here on in so pat yourselves on your backs
because you've made it. To be honest I rather enjoyed today.
Three painters who enjoy fucking about is a beautiful thing to
behold. Two isn't enough but three is perfect because that way
nobody gets on anyone else's tits for too long. Once again that's
science. If you work with someone for years and years for forty
hours a week you will know each other inside and out. It's like
having a brother or a sister and often you'll see them more than
your own bird or fella and this has its ups and downs. For me ten
years has always been the maximum I can handle however much
I love working with them after ten years they get on my tits and
we part ways. Still mates but from a safe distance because once
you're comfortable with someone all the politeness goes out of
the window it's like a marriage in which suddenly you both stop
trying and can't be arsed to put up with it anymore so one day

you go out for fags and never come back. Three painters is perfect because there's a fire wall. More than three is too many because then it becomes like an office environment and everyone is gossiping about everyone especially if they aren't confident in their abilities. Fuck knows if this is the same in all working environments but in the building game that's how it is. I know two chippies who work together all the time but one was married to the other ones sister and he fucked off with another bird and now they don't talk. They still work together because they run a business together but they never talk unless it's job related. It's ducking hilarious. It's like when a couple get divorced but due to the ridiculous price of houses they have to carry on living together because nobody can afford to move out. I don't think that either of these two lads have had to endure having to listen to the other one get shagged im the next room by another Chippie though. Oh yeah the gym! I've not been that much lately because there's still loads of chocolate to be eaten from Christmas and even though it's just the shit ones I'd rather munch through them while watching TV and being warm than piss about trying to stave off death by running and jumping about like some sad loser. To get through January you must get a bit self-indulgent and let yourself off the hook a bit or you're never going to make it out alive. That's boffin talk. I've done all the research so you don't have to. You eat and drink and sit about all you want and then suddenly it's February and you're on the clear because after this beautifully short month it's March and March is all about spring bulbs coming up out of the ground and sun kissed birds flying back home and loads of other optimistic shit. I did go yesterday though and it was nice to see the same old familiar faces. Chewing gum was there with his 'guess how old I am!?' Young people's trainers on grunting away like an absolute twat and upside down dwarf boy was there and when he saw some fit looking girl he immediately started walking about on his hands. It was both cringe and up to and including, ick.

There was also a new guy who was so over weight he couldn't walk probably and his trainers were all caved in. He staggered past me dripping in sweat and launched himself onto the rower and started manically rowing and I thought that we was going to die so I quickly fucked off in case I had to deal with giving him the kiss of life or that heart thing I've been meaning to get around to knowing for about thirty years now. I was glad I went because I didn't feel so guilty as afterwards I automatically got stuck into those coconut chocolate fuckers that nobody needs or wants and those chocolate strawberry mother fuckers that Satan must have invented. Christmas seems a million years ago now and when people wish me a happy new year I wonder what the fuck they are on about. Dickheads it's nearly Easter. Easter eggs already in the shops which I personally love because Easter means spring and lambs and warmer temperatures and lighter mornings. Oooh look at that I've cheered myself up. I never edit these and bang them out in a thrice so if there's any typos you're going to just have to deal with them as best you can. Nobody will read all this bollocks though so I might go back and slip in a few c words just for los shits unt giggles as the Italians say.

All ginger people look alike when they're asleep.

Ginger people are lovely and the female ones are really beautiful and the male ones have super long penises and most importantly when they are asleep they all look completely different.

Sexy gym stories part 100 New Year special.

I ain't going to lie I've been eating a shit load of food and drinking alcohol for the first time in years these past two weeks. I bought my dad a bottle of whisky for Christmas recommended by some client who was a bit of a whisky boffin or whatever they're called. I hear single malt and ten years old and Smokey and peaty and that'll do me so I bought the fucker a bottle and then I thought fuck it I'm an adult I'll get myself one and promptly did.

I waited until Christmas Day around noon and cracked it open. It smelled like medicine but when I passed it around the family we all agreed it smelled like wet dirt. Usually I like to shoot this kind of shit but now I'm 53 I decide to savour the taste and sip it while nodding appreciatively and saying connoisseur things like mmm Oaky and hint of pine needles? Oooh grassy! ... Herbal with a suggestion of ripe bell-end.

... After about ten seconds of this bollocks I got bored and shot it. Ten minutes later I cranked up the karaoke microphone and I was living the ruddy dream, pissed as a drunken fart. The clean pissed of someone who hasn't eaten but I had the voice of an angel - in my head anyway- when I sing I do the classics the dead rock and roll king, the dead crooner, the other dead crooner some Irish, stuff Christmas carols, blues, indie stuff, matey the dead guy and that other dead guy who died around Christmas either two years ago or ten years ago oh yeah and that other dead guy it's difficult when you're not allowed to mention celebrities but you get the idea I love to sing just for my own enjoyment it's good for your mental health if you don't sing I suggest giving it a bash but top tip use the echo function because the echo function is your friend you could flick a cat's nuts and as long as you've got the echo function ramped up said cat will sound like an angel. Anyway I dragged the family along with me and before you know it we were all a bit Brahms and sounding like the fucking Walton's Christmas special even the one who refuses to sing was singing it was beautiful whoever tells you that drugs are bad needs to drink a quarter of a bottle of whiskey turn up the volume to 11 and alienate your neighbours for years to come. Happy days. The best thing about Christmas is that it's the only time it's politically correct to have a handful of celebrations and a can of larger for breakfast and for a couple of days this is all well and good but it's not a long term strategy because sooner or later your liver will get up and walk out in disgust so in between this madness I've been trying to slip down the gym and try and ward off type two diabetes. Traditionally even your personal trainer geezers take it easy around this type of year but one of the guys in my gym didn't get the memo because he was looking extra buff and the fading fake tan his was sporting suggested to me that he'd just entered some kind of body building contest now me and him don't really get along that well his fault obviously because I'm a nice guy but when I say hello to someone two or three times and get blanked you're dead to me but as it was Christmas and we were both naked in the changing room I thought fuck it and asked him if he'd just been to a competition, ten seconds later he was showing me all his photos on his phone of him I'm a little pair of swimming trunks and telling me about his diet and this and that and I was lamenting the fact that even though his body was unbelievable sculptured his boat race and his thick bins left a lot to be desired although I guess this stopped my cock getting hard which was some kind of compensation. It's very rare that someone has the full package of good body and good face I guess that's why models get paid so much because it's so unusual most people are just average and if they've got a good body it's usually to compensate for something that's lacking. Ginger hair, a tiny cock, moody boat race -I don't make the rules so calm the fuck down ... Especially a lack of height. There's a guy who goes to my gym who walk on his hands up and down the gym and when he gets back to his feet he always looks around for some kind of appreciation or applause but everyone else in the gym without exception makes sure they're looking the other way because it's dickish behaviour and even though his body his pretty good and he ain't even a bad looking fucker he's short so all his tricks are meaningless and all they do is shout, I'm short! Look how insecure I am about my height! Who wants to see me juggle? Nope. I'll do a one hand press-up! Nah mate you're all good cheers. Look at my tall hair! It sticks right up! I will eat fire! Lock me inside a box and throw me in the fucking river and watch my escape! Let it go little dude or join the circus because we don't give a fuck.

In other news chewing gum won't stop groaning and grunting every time he lifts anything including the lid on his expensive water bottle especially if there's any women in the place they aren't pensioners and lemon ass keeps forgetting that he likes me now so I have to warm him up again every time I see the prick ... how come I can remember that he used to wank off over Valerie Singleton but I'm new to him every single time he sees me and the only thing he remembers I'd that he doesn't like I'll never understand.

Oh yeah yesterday I went for a walk with one of the step kids and his missus and at one point we got separated and I went from being some kind of loving paternal figure out with the kids to some kind of sex case loner within seconds who's just waiting for the chance to bum all the local kids. Couples were giving me evils and changing direction and hiding their ugly gargoyle brats and squirting mace in my face and calling me all sorts of unsavoury names and it was so horrifying I had to phone him and stay on the phone until they'd found me and I was shouting at passers-by , see? I'm not a nonce I just went a different way and got lost! You two tell them I'm not a sex case! Fucking exhausting. It's worth getting into a relationship just so you can go for a walk without ending up stoned to death.

Anyway the whole point of this rambling bollocks was to tell you that as we were on our way back we were waking up this big concrete path and a little kid of about three or four came scooting down towards us and he looked like a miniature man all gypsy haircut and suit which initially I thought was cute in a kind of ironic way then as he got closer he shouted move out of the way! In this little self-important way while giving me a very rude and dismissive look.

Now I can make a kid cry with one of my 'fuck you son, your mum may think you're the bollocks but you're just another little upstart spoiled wanker to me' type stares and I shot him one but it just bounced off the little runt. Did you see that cheeky little prick!? I enquired to my companions. What a little dick head said the bird one but the step kid one didn't see so we all turned around and I said, him! And pointed and just as we all turned he came off his scooter at speed and burst into tears and we all pissed ourselves as we saw his face break his fall. It was hilarious as we watched his shit parents waddle their way to their little cherub. Instant karma gonna get you immediately started to play in my head.

Please remember that the only people that think your kid is anything other than just another gobby little wanker is you and possibly their Nan and spoiler alert ... she thinks they're a massive twat as well.

Happy New Year

For people of a certain age you'll remember the delightful chimps tea party held at London zoo what a hoot seeing these little guys dressed up in human clothes and eating tea and biscuits or whatever the fuck they did but anyway it turns out they all had electric shock collars around their necks in case they misbehaved. Kinda takes the age off. I'm too scared to find out if the teabag advert chimps had the same treatment. Humans need a good hard slap sometimes.

When I was a child we all pronounced Boudicca 'Boudicca' but these days if you don't pronounce it 'Boudicca' you get laughed at. I'd loved to know the exact time when this change in pronunciation was made. Same with football commentators suddenly calling Milan 'Milan' the wankers. I'm old school and will always pronounce Boudicca as 'Boudicca' and Milan as 'Milan'. So bollocks. Or 'Bollocks' as we used to say.

Sexy gym stories Christmas spectacular.

On Monday morning off I went to the gym all chipper looking forward to my traditional two weeks off as a member of the building community. I know all these new-fangled young mother fuckers will be saying cor blimey guv two weeks!? Fuck me I'll be working right up until ten o'clock Christmas Eve night and back in 5am Boxing Day and blah, blah, blah well I couldn't give a fuck son/love/ them/they I've done all that and fuck that it's not for me anymore. I like to sit the fuck down and not know what the fucking day is and then come out the other side of Christmas all bright and breezy and ready to get stuck back in for another year.

So yeah I get to the gym and my heart is racing like fuck for some reason and I think I'm going to keel over but I crack on because I don't know what else to do. I go through reception make my platitudes and head down to the changing room full of dread and apprehension thinking that the best thing I can do is run it all away. I get changed and jump on the cross trainer. The lights are making me feel like I want to throw up and the fucking music that they constantly play is making me tense as fuck but I'm here now and I start the fucker up. What If I faint? There's only two people in here. What If I faint and piss myself? What if I faint, bang my head, piss and shit myself and wake up twenty years later in a hospital bed and everyone has a hover board but me and my wife has fucked off with one of the hospital warders who was supposed to be looking after me but has ended up banging my missus while I sat in a bed hearing every sound but not being able to do anything about it? But baby it was twenty years I have needs!? Fuck you baby. I pull out all the wires and stuff and head out into the new world to get me a hover board and a couple of hover prossies. I try my best to calm myself but I have a very vivid imagination and normally this is a good thing but at moments like this it's the opposite thoughts are flying through my skull different scenarios are being played out. I decide to get off the cross trainer but it's at an odd time and even though I'm not in my way OCD this is unsettling me. 14.58? I can't get off now that's mental! But I need to get off I can't be here forever. Eventually I go for it after deciding that the chest press is my friend and I'll be safe there. I jump off the cross trainer get a wet wipe and wipe it down then head for the chest press. I wipe it down and get under it. I feel better. The music though. That bass. The moronic words. Usually I don't mind it but right now it's cutting into me. I do a few lifts but I'm still jumpy as fuck. I faff about for a bit then decide to go. I dress quickly no shower no sauna. I get to the car and feel a bit better. While I'm concentrating on driving I feel ok but when I get home I feel mad as a hatter and think I'm going to have a heart attack. It was the start of a migraine.

Four days later it's subsided enough that I'm back down the gym this morning. I remember a few years ago my car started to overheat while driving home and when I stopped at the lights in wouldn't restart and it was a very dicey time I managed to restart it and chugged it out of harm's way but it took me six months to go that particular way home because of flashbacks and I didn't want to be scared to go back down the gym so I went today and after a nervous start I was fine. I even went into the sauna and as I lay there feeling normal again I reflected on the past few days and how nature will find a way to make you slow the fuck down. We used to get colds and flu but everything is sanitised all to fuck now so in my case on the first day of the holidays I got this fucking migraine. I think I used to get them as a kid that's what my mum said anyway but you can't trust her but I do remember the sensation and the nausea so maybe she was right. Fuck knows. As I was leaving the pool area and making my way back to the changing rooms for some reason there was a lot of people milling about in the sort of no man's land bit and as I was practically naked and freshly shaved And they all had their winter clobber on I felt a bit vulnerable. There was kids and adults and fuck knows what else and they were all just staring at me without fucking telling me why they were there and explaining what the utter fuck was going on it was all rather disconcerting so I said to nobody in particular, we'll this isn't sinister as fuck at all now is it? Not a murmur out of anyone so I put my head down and made my way pronto to the male changing rooms. More men and boys wearing over shoes were piling through and pushing past me but once I got through the door the sight of naked old men and their big old saggy ball bags and tiny cocks shuffling their way to the showers but me at ease and as these other fuckers filed past me I looked around and said with utter glee, crucifixion? First on the left!

And that's when I got what i crave more than anything else in this world, giving someone a good old fashioned belly laugh. I basked in that beautiful moment until one man chuckled, well it is a funeral! Which kind of took the edge off. Nobody expanded on that statement and I'm sat here wondering what the fuck he meant by that. Who has a funeral in a gym? Was it someone's last wish that all his or her or them or they's friends and family would pile into the changing rooms and mill about for a bit? Fuck knows and I'll probably never know but I got my laugh so I couldn't give a fuck.

Yeah so this one is about Remembering to take some time out to take care of yourself because if you don't nature will find one way or another to knock you on your arse.

To the members of the boring group,
Merry Christmas and a happy new year
Lots of love from Dom. X 😁 ♠ ♥ □

I'll tell you what, secret Santa is a bit of a let-down when you're self employed

If you burp while giving oral pleasure to a Japanese person, it's regarded as a compliment. I'm not sure about farts. Probably not. That's more of a German thing.

Printed in Great Britain
by Amazon

78683863R00119